KARMA, AG

(An Analytical Study of the

MW01328184

VIDHU JAIN

Contents

Page No.

Declaration i

Certificate ii

Certificate of Originality iii

Student Approval Form .... iv-v

Acknowledgement vi

Abbreviations viii

I Introduction 1-32

II Karma, Agency and Freedom in Jainism 33-66

III Karma, Agency and Freedom in Early Buddhism 67-102

IV Karma, Agency and Freedom in Sāṃkhya-Yoga 103-126

V Karma, Agency and Freedom in Nyāya 127-148

VI Karma, Agency and Freedom in Advaita Vedānta 149-184

VII Conclusion 185-201

I

Introduction

Indian philosophical thought has centred around various themes including epistemological, metaphysical, linguistic, ethical and ontological concerns. Discussions on knowledge and its sources, nature and existence of God, ethical values, causation, liberation, reality, and creation can easily be found. The doctrine of *karma* has also been an integral feature of classical Indian thought. But as far as the problem of freedom of the agent is concerned as well as the conception of agent's relation to the theory of *karma*, one does not find a comprehensive and detailed discussion done. Often scholars have raised their concerns with regard to this problem but to the best of my knowledge no constructive elaborate studies have been produced. At the most fragmented discussions pertaining to this problem do exist. It may have been felt by scholars that the classical period in Indian philosophy was majorly concerned with the ways in which a person could transcend the cycle of birth and death to attain eternal bliss or realise God and so much could be found on 'freedom from' and not so much on 'freedom to'.[1]

---

1. By 'freedom from' I mean freedom from the world of bondage and rebirth (that gives rise to pleasurable and painful experiences) i.e. freedom from the shackles of past, present and future *karma*. The disposition of the agent to act and scope of freedom in relation to the causal network of *karma* is what we mean here by the term 'freedom to'. As far as studies on classical Indian thought are concerned, it has been the case that 'freedom from' has overpowered the 'freedom to' concept; here arises the need as well as scope for the exploration of the 'freedom to' aspect.

But this very attainment of freedom requires effort not only in terms of spiritual practice but also in the sense of ethically desirable actions being done by the doer or the agent. One can find the issues pertaining to actions and their rewards and punishments being highlighted by different systems of classical Indian philosophy, which thereby raise the concerns over agency of an agent. Classical Indian philosophical thought has put in considerable effort to construct and elaborate the doctrine of action *(karma)* to set a background for the critical importance and significance of one's being an agent of actions. Some schools like Nyāya have further gone into precise details of essentials of agency with a motive to capture the very essence of the mechanism of reward and punishment. Also, Indian philosophical systems have been keen to understand action because for most of them final release or freedom in the soteriological sense can be attained only by having an absolute, conscious and informed control over one's actions. And this is the reason why an action in the Indian context is not merely or purely an act but it is always tied with the intention of its performance as well as with the result that ensues from it. This is the reason why the theory of action in the Indian context is known by the name of *karma* theory and is unanimously accepted in schools of Indian philosophical thought, though they might differ amongst each other with regard to the nuances of *karma*. Some people describe *karma* theory precisely as 'what you soweth, so shall you reapeth'. Actions done by persons in the past and present life hold the key to their future in terms of birth, life span, status, experience of pleasure and pain, psychological, physiological and genetic makeup. Now, the question arises: if one is determined in so many different ways, does it really make sense to hold that a person is responsible for actions as well as its results? To put it in other words, if a person is so programmed that he/she will do according to the information fed without fail, then how do we make sense of responsibility? We ask this because it is said that one cannot be held responsible unless one is free to act otherwise. Is there any sort of freedom for action available to the agent given the background of *karma* theory? Indeed, when we talk about the agent in Indian philosophical thought, the concept of selfhood has to be looked into from Indian perspective to understand who the agent is.

I

Aim of the Research

The proposed study will focus on the nature and the function of the agent in the classical Indian tradition.This will take a three pronged approach where firstly I ask what is the nature of action accepted in these schools? Secondly, I aim to find who the agent is, i.e intentions, volitions and desires are to be ascribed to whom? Lastly, I ask whether freedom of action can be ascribed to the agent in the background of the *karma* theory? If this is so, how will this freedom be interpreted and what is its scope in classical Indian philosophical thought.

Since action is the very basis of human existence and experience, it is natural to want to explore the nature of the doer of actions. Understanding of actions done by the agent on the one hand and the implications of the results brought about by the performance of these actions on the other hand have an impact on the soteriological framework of any classical school of Indian philosophical thought. An agent's or a person's whole existence is explained by way of the actions done by them, intentionally or unintentionally throughout their life time. Actions done by an agent creates vibrational as well as potential futuristic tendencies which determine one's present life as well as future existences. So, an extreme insistence is placed on doing those sorts of actions which bring good results or no results at all.[2] Good or bad actions bring merit and demerit which binds one to the cycle of birth and death, whereas those actions which do not bring about any results are favoured and looked upto, for they pave the way for one's release/liberation.

This brings us to an understanding that action and its agent have a significant role for any school of Indian philosophical thought giving it a teleological or purposive character. An agent is defined in terms of a person or an individual (*jīva*) or something that performs an action or actions. So, the agency is the faculty or potentiality to do actions. This can be clarified with the help of an example, a fruit falls down from a tree. But such an action of the fruit cannot be said to be a true manifestation of agency proper as no conscious effort is made on the part of the fruit to fall on the ground. Now, compare this to someone plucking it from the tree. This can be called an action with an agent proper who

2. Performance of detached actions does not lead to the formation of *karmic* fetters.

brought it about. Thus, there is a difference in the agency of the insentient and the sentient beings. This research work aims to deal with agency only with regard to human beings as they alone are capable of willing, volition, desiring and translating them into performance of actions or controlling not to turn their desires into action (physical or vocal). The term which is most commonly used by Indian philosophical system to express agency is '*kartṛtva*'. This work is an attempt to explore the nature of agent and agency along with the sense of freedom available to the agent to perform actions.[3]

We do not find the freewill debate in the Indian philosophical tradition the way we find it in Western philosophical thought. However, we can say that classical Indian thinkers even though they may not have explored this problem from the intellectual point of view, have explored it from the practical point of view. They have been concerned about the problems of life where a person is seeking some sort of connection between what he gets with what he does not expect. The whole endeavour to rationally make sense of what sort of conditions bring about what effects in the wake of transcending the cycle of birth and death, leads to the finding that human beings are responsible for what they do. If they are responsible, are there any conditions which determine their responsibility? It has been accepted generally that the freedom to act on the part of the doer is a necessary condition for holding one responsible. But what sort of freedom is

3. Note I will not be taking up the question of the gender of the agent. I am aware of it and the question is a big one. I hope to work on it and address it later in some further work.

needed to satisfy that demand? A great amount of literature has gone into catering to this question.[4] Classical Indian thinkers have also been keenly interested to answer this question but they have adopted a different way to talk about it. They have taken the path of the doctrine of *karma* to enunciate the nature of responsibility and henceforth explain if any form of freedom is available to persons that makes then accountable for their deeds.

The word *karman* or *karma* is derived from the Sanskrit root word '*kṛ*' which means to do, to act, to bring about etc. However, the word has deeper meaning connected with the past conditions for the action as well as future course of events to be brought about by an action.

Earliest or the Vedic conception of *karma* referred to correct performance of ritualistic activity with a view to receiving the desired results. No moral value was attached to such an action. Eventually *karma* acquired larger meaning and came to signify any correct action having ethical implications. All classical Indian schools of thought believe in the doctrine of *karma* except the Cārvākas. These schools use this doctrine in order to explain and justify different occurrences or happenings found in world order. According to them, the root cause of bondage is *karma* and ignorance. However, each school also has a unique way of understanding *karma*. When we look at accounts of the theory of *karma*, we find that the version of *karma* differs from system to system in both

4. This is with regard to western discussions on freewill problem.

the orthodox[5] and heterodox[6] schools of classical Indian philosophy. Even the indologists and scholars, Indian as well as Western do not seem to hold the same line of interpretation of the doctrine of *karma*.

Since the theory of *karma* is a unique and characteristic feature of Indian philosophical tradition, it is important also to show some underlying assumptions that are common and that emerge among different schools that accept it. They are as follows:

i) The stream of life and consciousness as revealed in mundane existence is without beginning. No absolute beginning of this stream is conceivable. But from whatever point we start, we are compelled to assume under logical necessity that it has an earlier history without which no rational understanding is possible. Present actions are the result of previous actions, previous actions are the result of their previous actions and so on extending indefinitely backward. Whenever we find any reference to the beginning of creation, it inevitably means the beginning of a particular cycle of time and not the beginning of creation itself.

ii) The soul assumes a body due to its past *karma*.[7] The quality of the body, its term of existence and the experience of joys and sorrows through the

5. *Ṣaḍdarśana* — Nyāya, Vaiśeṣika, Sāṃkhya, Yoga, Pūrva Mimāṃsā, Vedānta.

6. Jainism and Buddhism.

7. There are exceptions. E.g.Buddhism. Otherwise it is commonly accepted that soul gets conjoined to the body due to past or previous life *karma*.

body are also due to prior *karma*. Varieties of planes of life and consciousness are due to *karma*.

iii) It is generally believed that *karma* has in its background an element of ignorance.

iv) Destruction of *karma* as thus understood is believed to lead to a state of freedom defined by the absence of worldly joys and sorrows which are the inevitable concomitant or resultant of *karma*.

The various difficulties that envitably results from the assumptions of the theory of *karma* are: it appears to be fatalistic and that it renders human effort inefficacious. It is deterministic. We are disposed to do what our previous *karma* disposes us to. When all our tendencies and dispositions are determined by the factors which are not in our control, how are we to be held responsible for what we do? Responsibility requires that a person while doing action is free, and is not coerced to make a choice or decision. But the theory of *karma* claims that whatever actions we do all are determined by our past deeds. On the face of it, this implies that the doer or *kartā* of an action is only symbolic and does not really have agential powers.

Another difficulty is in balancing two accounts of the *karma* theory when understood as given above. On the one hand accepting *karma* means accepting deterministic causality, thereby putting every action, every event into a cause and effect relationship. On the other hand, the scope of the exercise of freedom on the part of the doer. Therefore, we arrive at the age old debate between determinism and freedom.

Further, there is no consensus on 'who the agent is' in different schools of Indian philosophy. For some, self or *ātman* is the doer while for others self is only the enjoyer and not the doer.[8] But how can someone who is not the doer of actions, become the experiencer of the results of the actions? Some have treated the agent as merely collection of successive states of events. It is a matter of common understanding that when we talk about actions it necessarily implies reference to an empirical being, an embodied being that performs them. But according to the doctrine of *karma* this very embodied existence is dependent and is the resultant of the actions done in previous lives. This appears to be a riddle.

Also, the doctrine of *karma* is rooted in the faith that what a person gets in the form of pleasure or pain is deserved by them as the just retribution of their good or bad deeds. This means that identity of the doer and the experiencer is important. But how this identity is to be established over successive life spans is indeed a very difficult question that underlies the *karma* debate. It can be said to be unrealistic for the assumptions on which it works are not verifiable, and often God or fate is invoked to explain its retributive nature. Lastly, it seems that the acceptance of *karma* theory leads to the understanding that each one has to attain release for one

8. More on the latter can be found in the chapter on Sāṃkhya.

self. Therefore one should pursue the path of renunciation and turn inwards to attain freedom.

Looking at the various issues that are pointed above, it seems that throwing light on the nature of agent in the background of the doctrine of *karma* and its analysis will help us to understand the various intricacies underlying *karma* itself and the agent for no action is conceivable without *kartā* or the doer. And this will in turn throw light on the other related issues such as the freedom of the agent and responsibility. Thus, keeping in focus the aim of the present research I have concentrated on the nature of the agent in selected schools of classical Indian thought along with the scope of freedom that can be said to be available to the agent in choosing a path of action. This will further require the examination of the concept of the self in these schools as the individual self in its embodied form alone can be the agent. Freedom of will or action which is regarded as the prerequisite for ascribing responsibility will be dealt with. The question of personal identity over different lifetimes for fixing responsibility has not been taken up in this work in an elaborate manner as this would widen the scope of the present study considerably.

II

Methodology

This work undertakes an indepth study of the concept of the agent and freedom of action, as explained above, in some selected schools of classical Indian philosophy. All these schools accept agency and consider it as an integral part of their philosophical discourse. They are Jainism, Early Buddhism, Sāṃkhya-Yoga, Nyāya and Advaita Vedānta. My account will be an expository analysis. This research work is grounded on both the original texts of the concerned schools as well as the relevant secondary sources. The original texts that I have referred to are given in the chapters that examine the schools respectively.

To cover so many schools was itself a monumental work. I hope to include in further research the other traditions and parts of the included traditions, also with fairly interesting perspectives, that I was not able to include in this work. Before we go on, some clarification about the terms that will be used is needed. These terms belong to Western ethical discussions and may prove extremely useful in assessing views on freedom and determinism in the Indian context. Though I believe that this kind of assessment may not be completely adequate to represent the tradition in question, but it will be I believe, a good place to start and can be very helpful fordeeper understanding provided one is attentive to the problems such comparisons can cause. I will be particularly using three ethical ideas namely: incompatibilism, compatibilism and voluntarism.

In the popular accounts we generally find the compatibilist view being contrasted with the incompatibilist view on freedom for action that can be ascribed to the agent. Incompatibilists hold that freedom is not compatible with determinism.[9] There are two positions under this view. On one hand we have fatalism which altogether denies any scope of freedom for action. Everything for its supporters is absolutely predetermined.[10] On the other hand are the libertarians, who maintain that the agent is absolutely free from any determinism.[11] The compatibilists on the contrary accept that determinism can be in sync with freedom. Determinism is the view which says that whatever happens, happens necessarily under the influence of past events/causes, in such a way that nothing can happen otherwise. According to compatibilists, freedom is compatible with determinism because freedom is essentially the absence of constraints or coercion in the process of choosing an action. They accept that one's will determines one's choice of actions. While making such a choice one is free from external influences and limitations. This allows one to take responsibility of the actions performed, whether good or bad, praiseworthy or blameworthy.[12] Another understanding of freedom accepted with regard to the compatibilist set up is that at the time of choosing an action, there were alternatives to choose from. This implies that had the agent wanted, another choice could have been made rather than the choice actually made. This

9. Paul Edwards, (ed.) *The Encyclopedia of Philosophy*, Vol.2, London: Collier Macmillan Publishers, 1972, pp. 743-4.

10. As far as classical Indian philosophical thought is concerned, the known school of *Ājīvikās* is said to have believed in destiny in an absolutist sense and propagated fatalism (*Niyativāda*).

11. The Indian materialist school of *Cārvāka* is well known for denying the theory of *karma* i.e. any form of determinism. This view of theirs is known as accidentalism (*Yadṛchhavāda*) in opposition to fatalism.

12. www.informationphilosopher.com/freedom/compatibilism.html

hypothetical choice of alternatives can be differently viewed. In my assessment of the freedom for action in the selected traditions, I have used it in both the senses as the schools I have discussed follow compatibilism without distinguishing its two senses.

The concept of freedom that we seek to explore here as far as the theory of *karma* is concerned cannot be supported from the libertarian point of view for they (libertarians) do not even accept agent causation. Also, hard determinism renders an agent merely a part of the larger mechanism where there is no power ascribed to him to initiate activity, but is component to the events. The most considerate answer which seems to overcome the difficulties raised by the two incompatibilist views is compatibilism. It accommodates the freedom of the agent in the form of an action being determined by the agent himself without external influences. So, an agent is free in the sense of not being determined by anything outside himself i.e. absence of external coercion or force which hard determinism proposes, and determined in the sense that an agent is the cause of his own action. Also, this causation of action is understood in the sense of being willed by the agent or the intention determined action of the person. It is this sense of understanding of freedom which I think can be seen to give some sense of freedom to act in Indian philosophical thought in the background of certain determinations in the form of accumulated actions determining one's present existence. So, there is always a scope to alter the future by focusing on the intention which in turn should be disciplined by set of values chosen by an individual/agent.

Another term which I will be using is voluntarism. Mackie explains a voluntary action as "one that issues from and somehow carries out the agent's 'will', it results from and either fulfils or makes some appropriate moves towards fulfilling some intention".[13] Voluntarism is a version of compatibilism where the agent's 'will' is the sole determinant of the choice of their action.

In addition to these three terms, I further also want to clarify the senses in which the terms 'freedom from' and 'freedom to' would be used which were mentioned in the beginning of the introduction. It has been a general concern in Indian philosophical thought how life which is viewed in itself to be suffering can be transcended. How can one remove suffering and bondage? How can one achieve freedom from the cycle of birth and death? This amounts to transcending *saṃsāra*, in other words a state free from any impediments leading to rebirth in the world. Thus, 'freedom from' is used here in the metaphysical sense of total cessation of suffering and *karmic* bondage to realise or attain ultimate freedom. The other term introduced is 'freedom to' which is one of the major concern taken up in this work. Human beings existing in the midst of worldly life are said to be active. Activity on the part of agents brings in the question of responsibility for the acts committed. For agents to be responsible

13. J.L. Mackie, *Ethics: Inventing Right and Wrong*, USA: Penguin Books, 1983, p.208

for their actions, freedom to act is a necessary precondition. If one is simply coerced to do something then one may not be held responsible for the same. So, 'freedom to' is used in the sense of the agent's inclinations or tendencies to act and also as that the scope of freedom to act when the *karmic* world view is the accepted theory. To clarify further, by this term is intended the scope of freedom of action on the part of agent or doer who is bound by their own *karma*.

Thus, when I am discussing 'freedom to' I propose to explore whether the freedom of action is taken in the compatibilist sense or the other two for the schools of classical Indian philosophy whose study is undertaken.

III

Literature Review

The question of freedom to act on the part of the doer when one is determined by one's past *karma* has caught the attention of some scholars. They have tried to bring an understanding of freedom not in the sense of one being absolutely free from any sort of determinants (like dispositions and psycho-physical tendencies), but, with these determining factors, can we talk about freedom for action? In this regard, I want to cite views held by various scholars to explain the sense of freedom available to the doer of actions.

P.K. Mahapatra writes that the doctrine of *karma* is:

> individualistic and usually backward looking in respect of securing appropriate consequences which everyone is entitled to by virtue of his (past) actions. Actions of individuals have the causal efficiency of producing consequences, which the respective individuals have to enjoy or suffer. This is because the individual, who is endowed with the power of freedom of will, does all his actions by choice, so it is supposed and therefore responsible for the consequences they produce.[14]

He seems to have taken freedom of will as a given without any need to explore what that freedom consists in. Just because it is necessary to make sense of responsibility freedom is taken as a given which paves the way to rationalize what one gets as reward and punishment. Whether one is really free and if free then in what way are questions which cannot be settled with mere common sense explanation and must be addressed.

Sarvapalli Radhakrishnan in his book *An Idealist View of Life* writes:

> *Karma* is not so much a principle of retribution as one of continuity.....all things in the world are at once causes and effects. They embody the energy of the past and extend energy on the future. *Karma* or connection with the past is not inconsistent with creative freedom. On the other hand it is implied by it. The law that links us with the past also asserts that it can be subjugated by our free action. Though the past may present obstacles, they must all yield to the creative power in man in proportion to its sincerity and insistence.... The principle of *karma* has thus two aspects, a retrospective and a prospective continuity with the past and creative freedom of the self.[15]

14. P.K. Mahapatra, *Survey of Modern Writings on Classical Indian Ethics: Methodological Hints for Appraising as Ethics,* HSPC, Delhi: Motilal Banarsidass, Vol. XII part 2, 2012, p. 28.

15. Sarvapalli Radhakrishnan, *An Idealist View of Life,* London: Unwin Paperbacks, 1988, p. 125.

Radhakrishnan explains life with the help of a game of bridge. Cards are given to the player and they do not select them. One is more free when the game starts and later on when the game has developed their choices become restricted. But till the very end there is always a choice.

For him the "self is not free from the bonds of determination, it can subjugate the past to a certain extent and turn it into new course. Choice is the assertion of freedom over necessity by which it converts necessity to its own use and thus frees itself from it..." [16] He quotes Pāṇini that 'the human agent is free' (*Aṣṭādhyāyī* 1.4.54) and declares that "if there is no indetermination, then human consciousness is an unnecessary luxury." [17] So, Radhakrishnan clearly denies predestination and complete determinism in nature. He accepts that human beings have creative freedom by the use of which they can break the determinateness in the natural order and create possibilities. Human beings are capable of choices and will is nothing over and above or separate from the self but only its active side. He adds that the more a person is aware and in realization of the power of the self, the more the person can be said to be free.

Thus, Radhakrishnan can be said to accept freedom in the compatibilist sense. However, an elaborate argument in favour of this view cannot be found in his work. It seems that he takes a hasty approach to his conception of creative

16. *Ibid.*
17. *Ibid.*, p. 126.

freedom without giving enough explanation about the nature of the agent, his agency and freedom to act.

Another scholar S.N. Mahajan has tried to study freedom from an Indian perspective. He explores, in 'Freedom: An Indian Perspective', the idea of what constitutes freedom and how to ascribe responsibility, and claims that it is not merely freedom in the negative sense of absence of external constraints. For him, the negative sense of freedomis not a sufficient one and one must look towards the absence of or presence of internal constraints, inner compulsions to supply the full conditions of freedom.[18] He says "in fact in so far as the internal compulsions are more subtle and elusive but forge a formidable vice-like grip on man, any analysis of freedom which leaves out an understanding of these factors will necessarily remain superficial."[19]

To argue for the same Mahajan brings in the theories of psycho-analysis and psycho-therapy to talk about inward reflection and attainment of freedom in the sense of overcoming one's attachments and disentangling the roots of the ego based life with its worry, anxiety and dualities. The energies of the psyche having been liberated from the clamping, constraining hold of the ego and there is a natural flow of free, spontaneous activity. He quotes psychologist, Hans Jacobsk and Jung, who have emphasized the importance of taming the mind to

---

18. S.N. Mahajan, 'Freedom: An Indian Perspective', *Concept of Man in Philosophy,* R.A. Sinari, (ed.) Shimla: Indian Institute for Advanced Studies, 1991 p. 114.

19. *Ibid.*, p. 115.

unlock its natural powers by concentration and observing one's own thoughts. Whatever lies dormant deep in the conscious should be dug out and released. This enhances one's real freedom. Mahajan concludes with the idea that real freedom consists in the realization of one's identity with the self which is the pure subject, the witness and substratum of all states of consciousness. The more one's activity becomes spontaneous and less coerced from external factors, the more choices made by oneself become free. Thus, he also tries to carve space for freedom in the background of psychic determinants where there is a possibility to transcend the so called negative tendencies or ego generated vices to see one's real self. This very reflection brings real freedom and spontaneity in one's activity where one not only transcends external constraints but also inner constraints.

Another somewhat close view to Mahajan's is of Kalidas Bhattacharya. He writes in 'The Status of the Individual in Indian Philosophy' that the "law of *karma* as understood to be against freedom of action is not so".[20] According to it only birth *(jāti)*, age *(āyuh)* and experience of pleasure and pain for an individual *(bhoga)* are determined. Actions at the moral and spiritual levels are not. He cites three reasons for that: firstly, merit and demerit one accrues from previous life gets exhausted by producing appropriate results in the form of pleasurable or painful experiences in present and future births. The merits and

---

20. Kalidas Bhattacharya, 'The Status of Individual in Indian Philosophy', *Philosophy East and West,* Hawaii: University of Hawaii Press,Vol.14, 1964, pp. 134-135.

demerits do not accrue further results as this would make the cycle endless. Secondly, if one is so tightly tied in the chain of cause and effect where good and evil deeds done in one life leads to good and evil results respectively in the other, this would amount to saying that there is no scope of improvement on the part of the doer or experiencer. This sort of complete determinism is not accepted in Indian thought. Lastly, the above stated determinism will render the observance of ethical actions useless as one cannot change the succession of events. Thus, attaining liberation becomes impossible.[21]

Bhattacharya points out that spiritual actions which proceed from detachment have maximum freedom because there is no blind submission to attachment (*rāga)* and hatred *(dveṣa)*. Moral actions distinguishing the performatory and prohibitory actions are free in the sense that there is always a possibility of not having done the wrong and consciously chosen the right actions in consonance with one's value system. So, there is always scope of free action according to Bhattacharya at the level of spiritual and moral actions for the doer always has a choice. This implies that he also gets into the discussion of necessity of freedom by way of which he establishes that there is freedom to act.

Karl Potter has tried to approach this problem from a different perspective. In 'The *Karmic*: Apriori in Indian Philosophy', he experiments with the idea of apriori, and asks if it is applicable in Indian philosophy or not like the Kantian

---

21. *Ibid.*

apriori. By apriori is meant "a statement or a proposition embedded in an interpretative scheme the structure of which is internally necessary, such that the relations among its constituents are fixed in advance of its application."[22] Potter explains that though we cannot have an apriori in Indian philosophy the way some western scholars like Kant have shown, some of its general features can be noticed in Indian philosophy. He says that "the general assumption governing the Indian account is that our concepts are generated by our *karmic* inheritance and that within the limits of the theory of *karma* it can be manipulated, revised or exchanged for something else."[23] He develops a very sophisticated understanding of determination of one's present conceptual construction and interpretative scheme by one's past *karmas*. Thus, according to Potter, "*karmic* apriori is not the limitations of human reason which determine the categories of interpretation that we use, it is rather those habits of mind that have been generated from the past lives."[24] These habits are an outcome of two kinds of conditioning factors; dispositions *(vāsanas)* and traces *(saṃskāras)* from past lives called *karmic* residue. This sort of *karmic* apriori is both fixed and revisable: fixed in the sense of fructification of previous *karma* without any variations and revisable in the sense that one can attempt to condition one's future dispositions. Thus, one can improve one's interpretations morally and

22. Karl H.Potter, 'The *Karmic*: Apriori in Indian Philosophy', *Philosophy East and West,* University of Hawaii Press, Vol. 42, 1992, p. 407.

23. *Ibid.*, p. 413.

24. *Ibid.*

spiritually and attain a better place in next life and a truly wise man should curb all his interpretations altogether.

Potter in another writing brings a significant development with regard to the problem of the mutual understanding between freedom and determinism in Indian context. He explores that the belief in the law of *karma* and transmigration doesnot necessarily end up in fatalism in the work titled 'Freedom and Determinism: An Indian Perspective'.

The form of determinism described by Potter does not preclude freedom, if by freedom is meant the ability to channel our actions in the directions we intend, coupled with the capacity for growth, for acquiring new abilities. There is a difference between calling it deterministic and determinate. When an agent tries to do something and succeeds, two events are fully determinate what an agent did when tried and succeeds in doing. What is not determinate is the effort and intention. The effort consists of a determinate event considered under a determinable description. This determinable description is produced by the very nature of the agent's abilities. Thus effort is a result of conditions jointly sufficient to produce a determinate event along with the sufficient condition to produce the ability to intend certain determinable range of events as outcomes of the actions. To say that the agent has an ability to x or not-x , it does not follow that he has the ability to x, say, which precludes an ability to not-x, even though x and not-x are themselves mutually exclusive alternatives. To use Potter's words, "Abilities can be viewed as selective mechanisms, distinguishing a range of events according to a disjunction of relevant features." [25] To clarify, it is not that dispositions are uncaused, rather they are determinable without being determinate. In the Indian context, blind submission to emotions involves the production of relatively determinate actions by relatively determinate causes. Where effort or trying comes into the picture, there enters an element of selection and choice. Freedom, according to the Indian view, consists, according to Potter, in enriching the scope of one's abilities so that one is minimally dependent upon determinate passions produced by external events not of one's choosing. The detachment recommended in Indian thought is the broadening of one's responsive awareness simultaneously with development of non-dependence on external passions.

The view of Potter has been helpful to explore the conception of freedom that is dealt in the proceeding work but it does not clarify the sense of freedom as understood in different systems of Indian thought.

Johannes Bronkhorst in his paper 'Free Will and Indian Philosophy' discusses the problem of freewill. For him in the classical Indian tradition the issue of freewill against determinism is merely apparent than real. He writes:

> the question of free will is not an issue, because there is no place for a felt contradiction between decisions and the mechanism that

---

26. K.H. Potter, 'Freedom and Determinism: An Indian Perspective', *Philosophy East and West,* Vol.17, 1980, p.121

> makes humans act; there is no place for such a contradiction because human mental activity plays a crucial role in the process. Determinism, seen this way, takes nothing away from the freedom to act in accordance with one's feelings, because these feelings are themselves part of the mechanism described.[26]

Bronkhorst sees human experiences and functions as part of the mechanical process. Within this there exist human feelings and emotions which are not reducible to physical or mechanical processes. In other words, there is no friction between free will and determinism. Bronkhorst has utilized Nyāya-Vaiśeṣika's psychological explanation of performance of actions by an agent. There are various conditions involved in this process where one of the important conditions is the desire to do an action which is the result of previously experienced pleasures. This sort of activity is the internal mechanism of the agent who is a part of the Nyāya-Vaiśeṣika psychology. He writes:

> Nyāya-Vaiśeṣika psychology then, is the kind of psychology in which the conflict between conscious will and determinism does not arise, because even if we think of it in deterministic terms, this does not deprive humans of the possibility to act in accordance with their will. To repeat it once more: free will is not an issue in Nyāya-Vaiśeṣika because its psychology uses experiential terms among its fundamental notions. [27]

Apart from these views on freedom of the agent, more recently a collection of essays by different authors examining the interplay of freewill and agency along with the understanding of selfhood in various schools of classical Indian thought

27. Johannes Bronkhorst, 'Free Will and Indian Philosophy', *Antiqvorvm Philosophia*, Vol.6, Rome: Fabrizio Serra Editore, 2012, p.24

28. *Ibid.*

has been edited by Matthew Dasti and Edwin Bryant.[28] This work is to the present date the only consistent attempt to unravel the importance of comprehending the nature of self, its characteristics for the understanding of agency in particular schools of classical Indian thought. Discussions on freewill are not explicitly done but somehow woven into the explanation of the different aspects of agency. Some writers in this anthology have also incorporated the debates amongst Indian schools to give comparative accounts of self and agency. Though this is a remarkable work, I feel the discussion of theory of *karma* for the development of agency is important and inevitable and needs to be worked on additionally. Also, the questions pertaining to freedom of the will can be raised when there is this assumption in the background that one is determined in so many different ways (determined by one's *karma*). Moved by this sort of understanding of the issue, I have endeavoured to explicitly handle the concerns of freedom for action and location of agency as they emerge from the theory of *karma*.

Wendy Doniger O'Flaherty while summarising the historical origins of the *karma* theory in her book '*Karma and Rebirth in Classical Indian Traditions*' brings in the featrures of the theory of *karma* which has been summed up in the following words:

---

29. Matthew Dasti & Edwin Bryant, (ed.) *Freewill, Agency and Selfhood in Indian Philosophy*, New York: Oxford University Press, 2014.

> we mustered our courage to attempt the definition (of *karma*) again, and came up with several possible formulations. The general consensus that we were dealing with a theory of rebirth based on the moral quality of previous lives was further refined by A.K.Ramanujan(A) and Charles Keyes(B). The essential constituents of a *karma* theory are: (A) (i) causality (ethical or non ethical, involving one life or several lives). (ii) ethicization (the belief that good and bad acts lead to certain results in our life or several lives). (iii) rebirth. (B) (i) explanation of the present circumstances with reference to previou sactions, including (possibly) actions prior to birth; (ii) orientation of present actions towards future ends, including (possibly) those occurring after death. (iii) moral basis on which action past and present is predicated.[29]

This whole discussion about the *karma* theory clarifies that in which ever aspect we understand it there is an essential involvement of human agency. Agent is the inevitable component of this theory without which there can be no value attached to it. Actions are performed by the agent and their results are also borne by them. So, agent is the locus of both the performance of actions and the experience of the results of actions. Though it gives an exhaustive account of theories of *karma* and rebirth in Classical Indian Philosophy and from that point of view is very valuable. However, it says very little about the agent.

A candid and a critical take on the mitigation between the *karma* theory and the scope of freewill is done by Balasubramaniam.[30] He vehemently challenges the assumption accepted generally by all schools that there is strict conformity

---

29. Wendy Doniger O'Flaherty, *Karma and Rebirth in Classical Indian Traditions*, Delhi: Motilal Banaridass, 1980, p. xi.

30. R. Balasubramanium, 'The Theory of Karma and the Philosophy of Advaita', *Indian Philosophical Quaterly*, Vol.6, 1978-79, p.567-9.

between the actions done in one life and the results borne from them in another life. He does this on two grounds, firstly, the problem of evidence for this claim and secondly, the lack of remembrance by the soul of the continuity of its transition from one life to another life. For the first claim, he says we find no demonstrative proof of the existence of an immortal transmigrating soul and therefore, this claim can be reasonably disputed. Further, for the second claim he says that the soul is ignorant for what it suffers. This is as if one is punished without any awareness of what it is punished for. This he finds to be unjustifiable as this ignorance deters one to forbid oneself from committing more evil.

Balasuramaniam finds a somewhat satisfying solution to this problem in Advaita Philosophy; nonetheless, he says it to be elusive. By maintaining the soul (*jīvātmā*) to be nothing but the ultimate (*Brahman*) itself, the sufferings that the soul experiences are self inflicted rather than any external mechanism or entity playing a role in doing it. This suffering is due to ignorance of the above mentioned truth. He interrogates "...why should *Paramātmā* [*Brahman*] take to such a course of action, when it lacks nothing and needs nothing?"[31]

Even though this is one of the perennial problems shooting up from *karma* theory, the focus of the present work is different. Here the point of discussion is the individual self (embodied being) and the understanding of its agency aspect.

31. *Ibid.*, p.569.

The ambit of my research is to deal with this aspect along with the question of freedom for action at the empirical level.

Peter Harvey, a contemporary scholar of Buddhist philosophy, in a recent work entitled 'Psychological versus Metaphysical Agents: A Therāvāda Buddhist view of Free-Will and Moral responsibility' has dwelled upon the nature of agency in Therāvāda Buddhism. He writes:

> At MN.III.179, 180 it is said that Yama, king of the dead, reprimands an evil-doer arriving in hell, saying that a certain deed was done by him, and not by any friend or relative, so that he must experience its *karmic* result. This passage need not imply that such a past action was done by a substantial, still existent Self, but only that it was done by an earlier portion of the stream-of-states that the person now is, rather than by any other stream-of-states. 'He', no one else is responsible. This shows that agency of, and responsibility for actions is accepted in Therāvāda Buddhism.[32]

Harvey explains that the agent who performs actions is subject to change and is distant from any abiding, unchanging, unconditioned entity. The agent is coiled up as an enmeshed entity and as an amalgamation of network of conditions, like all conditioned beings which are non-Self. He points out that it is implausible to ascribe actions, changes and doer-ship to a permanent self which as said is unchanging and unconditioned. He goes on to say:

> One might like to think that the agent of one's actions is an essential, permanent Self/I-agent, but this in fact makes no sense if taken literally. Yes actions are done by the kind of person one has

32. Peter Harvey, 'Psychological versus Metaphysical Agents: A Therāvāda Buddhist view of Free-Will and Moral Responsibility', *Buddhist Perspectives on Free Will: Agentless Agency?*,(ed.) Rick Repetti, Routledge, 2016,p.159

> been so far, but this is 'permanent' only in an approximate sense, as a cluster of mental and physical process events with a reasonably consistent, but still changeable, pattern to it. This is the only kind of thing that can be an agent of action, and Buddhism does not, and has no reason to, deny its reality... So while the Therāvāda suttas do not accept a permanent Self that is the agent of action, that stands above all conditions, unaffected by them, a will that is unconditioned, totally free, or 'strong free will', it does accept that a person, as a cluster of conditioned processes including will, can have agency and responsibility.[33]

Various scholars have explored the issue of agency in the absence of a permanent abiding self along with freedom and responsibility covering Therāvāda and other Mahāyāna traditions. But I have tried to study these issues only in the context of *Nikāyas.*

So, it can be summed up that in the classical Indian tradition generally there is acceptance of the determination of one's present state of existence by previous *karma*. It is also unanimously accepted that this determination is not endless and there is scope of improvement to one's present as well as future state of existence. Elaborate discussions on prohibitions and prescriptions are found. But one rarely finds any attempt where constructive analysis of agency is done from the point of view of the different schools of classical Indian thought which could pave the way for the discussion of freedom to action and relate it with the issue of responsibility. This is what I am humbly hoping to add.

---

33. *Ibid.*, pp.160-61.

IV

Chapterisation

The thesis shall be divided into five chapters apart from an introduction and a conclusion. Each chapter will be devoted to a selected school of Classical Indian thought. I have chosen Jainism, Early Buddhism, Sāṃkhya-Yoga, Nyāya and Advaita Vedānta for the discussion. Each chapter shall be divided into three sections where section I will raise questions addressing the theory of *karma* or action, section II will discuss agency and finally section III will look at the possibility of freedom for action within that system.

The first chapter 'Karma, Agency and Freedom in Jainism,' will focus on how the *jīva* (empirical self) is the agent, doer, knower as well as the experiencer who attracts different *karma* particles towards itself by way of mental, bodily and speech acts. It is interesting to note that Jainas, on the one hand, accept *karma* in the form of material particles that are drawn towards the self to form a veil hiding its infinite nature. On the other hand, they accept that the self is perfect, possessed of infinite qualities. The question then arises as to how a conscious self can stir this matter to be pulled towards itself. The answer to this question requires an understanding of the nature of *karma* and agent in Jainism. This is what my chapter will be centrally looking at. My assessment intends to further throw light on the issue of autonomy of the individual self to transform itself and absolve itself of all *karmic* matter.

The second chapter, 'Karma, Agency and Freedom in Early Buddhism,' shall be focussing on the analysis of the nature of agent according to early Buddhism with special reference to Pāli *Nikāyas*. Buddhism does not believe in the permanence of anything including the denial of a permanent self (*anattavāda*). They accept that intentional action is *kamma*. Now, if there is no abiding entity that is the locus of intention or volition, how is action to be explained? This question stresses the need to understand the nature of agency in the absence of eternal self. Also, in the absence of a permanent entity how is responsibility to be understood. This in turn requires the discussion of freedom of action in Buddhism. So, the central focus of this chapter is the Buddhist understanding of the agent and the idea of freedom that emerges from this understanding.

The third chapter, 'Karma, Agency and Freedom in Sāṃkhya-Yoga', will be exploring the conception of agency from the Sāṃkhya-Yoga perspective. They accept two mutually exclusive and independent realities: *puruṣa* and *prakṛti*. *Puruṣa* is conscious, eternal, inactive and immutable while *prakṛti* is material, unconscious and dynamic. If *puruṣa* is conscious but inactive and *prakṛti* is unconscious but dynamic then how does activity take place? And who is the agent? These are interesting questions that will be investigated in this chapter. Apart from this question I shall also be looking at the possibility of the freedom of the agent in Sāṃkhya-Yoga philosophy.

The fourth chapter, 'Karma, Agency and Freedom in Nyāya,' shall be exploring the arguments advanced by the Naiyāyikas to show that the individual self is the doer. They accept self as a substance capable of possessing qualities where even consciousness is not its essential quality but merely adventitious. When the self is devoid of consciousness then what leads to the manifestation of agency in the individual self will be assessed in this chapter. I will also be evaluating the question of freedom of action when on the one hand they accept the concept of unseen potency (*adṛṣṭa*) determining various aspects of one's existence and on the other hand support the performance of action by one's own will.

The fifth chapter, 'Karma, Agency and Freedom in Advaita Vedānta' enquires into the question of agenthood whilst acknowledging that the Advaitins accept the non- dual self to be the ultimate reality. Pertinent questions arise: who is the agent? Is it *Ātman?* Is it *Brahman?* Is it the cognitive faculty (*antaḥkaraṇa*)? Is it the individual self (*jīva*)? These series of questions are the prime focus of this chapter. Further, the abandonment of actions as the means to realize the non-dual self raises the essential question about the very existence of agency. This chapter thoroughly investigates the above mentioned questions to understand the nature of agenthood (if any) in Advaita thought.

The conclusion sums up the key points and specific nuances of each chapter looking at the various aspects of *karma*, agency and the freedom. Some pertinent findings will be highlighted.

II

Karma, Agency and Freedom in Jainism

This chapter aims to deliberate upon and assess the Jaina account of *karma,* agent and freedom to act. Jainism as an independent tradition is one of the oldest school of thought whose historicity can be traced back to atleast 9thcentury B.C. (which is the time period of the 23rd *Tīrthaṇkara* Pārśavnātha). Jainism as a living philosophy and religion recounts twenty four realized teachers (*Tīrthaṇkaras*) from whom this tradition is believed to have ascended from pre-historic times. They are believed to have conquered all their passions and desires to achieve liberation. A liberated soul is called an *Arhat.* In this school of thought attaining freedom in the soteriological sense is the ultimate aim of human life.

The Jaina philosophy accepts a dualism of self (*jīva)* and non-self (*ajīva),* animate and inaminate beings respectively. Both are accepted as substance (*dravya*) qualified by permanent (*guṇa*) and temporary (*paryāya*) qualities. The self is an eternal spiritual substance and is not material. It transmigrates from one birth in a body to another. Non-self is the material principle or matter (*pudgala*), the principle of motion (*dharma),* the principle of rest (*adharma*), space (*ākāśa*) and time (*kāla*).[1] Matter is either in the form of atoms (*pudgala*) or aggregates of atoms. These are homogeneous. The unique feature of this

1. Jadunath Sinha, *Indian Philosophy*, Vol. II, Delhi: Motilal Banarsidass, 1999, p. 180.

school is that nature of *karma* is also conceived to be atomic in nature (*paudgālika*) which is pervading the whole universe. Matter has its own independent existence like self, and in the form of atomic particles possesses touch, taste, smell and colour. These particles have the capacity to unite with certain physical laws to form aggregates (*skandhas*) which are heterogeneous in nature.[2] Further, there is no conception of creator God in Jainism. The world is eternally self-existent and has selves and material objects. In Jainism, reality is viewed or understood by anyone from different standpoints or views called *nayas*. Jainas believe that any substance or entity has innumerable aspects which can be known only partially from a perspective. One can be said to be in grasp of partial truth all the time till one attains omniscience (*kevalajñāna*). Otherwise, one can be said to possess only a relative knowledge of these innumerable aspects of an object or entity. Expressions of the relative truth by way of relative judgements constitute the Jaina theory of Seven-fold predication (*Syādvāda*).[3] The realization of one's knowledge and understanding of one's perception and cognition being relative forms the basis of Jaina ethics of *ahiṃsā*. Jainas propagate the attainment of liberation by sheer self-exertion. They say that each self is innately capable of liberating itself by completely destroying the veil of *karmic* matter that covers the infinite nature or capacities

---

2. H.V.Glasenapp, *Doctrine of Karma in Jaina Philosophy*, California: Asian Humanities Press, 2003, p. 25.

3. John E. Cort, 'Intellectual Ahiṃsā Revisited: Jain Tolerance and Intolerance of Others', *Philosophy East and West*,Vol. 50, (1), Hawaii, 2000, pp. 325-7.

of self like knowledge, power, bliss and perception. One who attains victory over the evils of passion and desire is called the conqueror (*Jina)*. The doctrines of *Anekāntavāda*, *Syādvāda* and *Ahiṃsā* together are the fundamental prerequisites for an agent (*jīva*) to realize emancipation.

The association of self and *karmic* matter in this world is eternal and inadvertently brings about agency to the individual self (*jīva*). Any *jīva* living in this world therefore cannot but be the doer of actions. These actions bring effects which result in bondage of the self. If actions bring about bondage and *jīva* cannot remain inactive then how can self ever realize its own innate nature i.e. freedom from bondage? This raises very legitimate questions like: what is the nature of *jīva* and how does *jīva* accumulate *karma* and if the *jīva* is bound or determined by their own *karma*, is there any freedom available to the agent (*jīva)* to elevate themselves from their state of existence as shackled in *karma*? An enquiry into the answers of these questions is relevant for any research on agency and freedom in Jaina philosophical thought. I shall be looking at *Āchārāṅga Sūtra* (AS), *Tattvārtha Sūtra* (TS) of Umāsvāti, *Samayasāra* (SS) of Kundakundācharya, for the understanding of Jaina conception of *karma,* agency and freedom. Apart from these texts I shall also rely on several secondary texts to arrive at the answers I seek.

I

Now after laying down the foundations, we deliberate upon the doctrine of *karma*. The doctrine of *karma* in Jainism is different from other parallel theories of *karma* in the sense that here it is understood as concealment obscuring the self-luminous nature of the self (*ātman*) with subtle matter. This subtle matter or *karma* which is driven towards the self is due to the "operation of the body, speech and mind".[4] It has a distinct quality of bringing about merit and demerit.This merit and demerit facilitates the association of each self with the matter. As a result of this association the self is said to be possessed of body, speech and mind.[5] The physical body (*kārmaṇśarīra*) houses both the speech and mind function. The functioning of these corporeal elements in individual beings (*jīva)* under the influence of nescience or ignorance produces knowledge and energy obscuring *karmas*. The self is said to be possessed of infinite knowledge and energy, however due to the operation of *karma* its qualities of knowledge and energy get restricted resulting in bondage (*bandha*).[6] The mind influences the function of speech and body. Here, the mind can be seen to be manifested at two levels, the physical (*acetnā*) and psychical (*cetnā*).[7] The physical mind is the brain which controls the activity of the body and speech

---

4. TS, 6.1, p.151, *kāya-vāṅ-manaḥkarma yogaḥ.*
5. TS, 5.19, p.130, *śarīra-vāṅ-manaḥ-prāṇā-pānāḥ pudgalānām.*
6. *Ibid.*
7. S. Radhakrishnan, *Indian Philosophy*, Vol.1, Delhi: Oxford India Paperbacks OUP, 2008, p. 265.

organ at the physical level and the psychical mind is the conscious aspect of the self which regulates the physical mind.[8] The psychical mind is responsible for the production of psychical states of desires, passions (*kaśāya*) and emotions in the self (*bhāva karma*) culminating in psychical/emotional bondage (*bhāva bandha*) whereas the physical mind leads to the activity of speech organs and body which attracts material particles (*dravya karma)* resulting in materio-physical bondage (*dravya bandha*). This implies that the *karma* itself attracts *karma.*[9] The attraction or the movement of the *karma pudgala* (*kārmanvargaṇā*) towards the self is called influx (*āśrava*) which is the cause of bondage (*bandha*). The psychical and physical *karmas* are tied to each other as cause and effect. The relation can be understood from their functioning. The psychical *karma* is the cause which brings the modification of material particles into effect which is material *karma*. This in turn makes the material *karma* the cause of the modification of the psychic *karma*. The soul is the substantive cause (*upādāna kāraṇa*) of its thoughts. The *karma* matter is the external cause (*nimittakāraṇa)*.[10] However, psychical which is the internal state and external which is the material state are mutually exclusive to each other. Both these states precede and determine each other externally.The meaning is that though there are two levels

8. TS, 5.19, p.130.
9. TR,v. 6.1.7, p. 504.
10. B.J. Jhaveri, 'Considerations of Self in Jaina Philosophy', *Mahavira and His Teachings,* Bombay: Bhagvan Mahavira's 2500th Nirvana Mahotsav Samiti, 1977, pp. 235-6.

of the operation of *karma*, they both function in a continuous cyclical process till the time the *karmic* influx is stopped.

After discussing all this, the fundamental question that can nonetheless be asked is that what is the reason in believing that the nature of *karma* is inherently material? An answer to this question can be traced in *Tattvārtha Sutra*[11] where it is clarified that *karma* produces pain. Pleasure, life, death etc. which are experienced by the self or agent in the form of bodily manifestations and this is why it is accepted as material in nature. Things or objects, made up of matter produce pleasureable and painful experiences. These experiences are an outcome of the fruition of the pleasure and pain giving *karmas* (*sātāvedanīya* and *asātāvedanīya karma*) and the co-related external conditions including objects. It must be noted that *karma* is an instrumental cause of this fruition while the principle cause is the self. *Karma* becomes potent to produce effects only in so far it is associated with the self (*jīva*) without which it stands meaningless. This is an ideal and theoretical position. In reality "The soul is eternally infected by matter; its union with the *karman* has no beginning and, as every moment it is gathering new matter, it has in the natural course of things, no ending".[12] Jainas explain that due to the beginningless association of the *karmic* matter with the self, it is qualified with the presence of passions namely greed, attachment, vanity and hatred. Due to this the soul is always vibrating.

11. TS, 5.20, p.131.

12. Glasenapp, *The Doctrine of Karman*, p. 3.

Presence of passions in the self keeps it vibrating attracting further new *karmic* matter which entangles the self.[13]

As it has been most often said that subtle *karmic* particles enter the self and contaminate its true nature. One can ask whether such an ingression is possible unless the self is made up of parts.[14] Also, how is it possible that something which is material in nature can influence and modify the non-material spiritual substance when both are of an entirely distinct nature? This objection has been answered with the help of analogies in Jaina texts. Just like the self who is essentially conscious can be intoxicated by the consumption of alcohol or drugs, similarly, the immaterial self is obscured by the material *karma*. This is possible because the empirical selves are in embodiment.[15]Another analogy to explain the same problem is that of the manifold medical effects that are observed in the body when a medicine is taken. In the same way the subtle *karmic* matter is capable of producing certain effect in the self (*jīva*).[16]

After analogically having explained above that material objects can influence the immaterial self and change it, another difficulty that arises is about how the union between these two opposite entities is established. The union of the two is explained as the mixing of the water with milkor heat uniting with the iron. In the

13. TS, 8.3, p.191.
14. M. Hiriyanna, *The Essentials of Indian Philosophy,* London: Allen and Unwin, 1951, p. 61.
15. Ashvin Desai, *Between Eternities,* Lincoln: Universe Publication, 2007, p. 138.
16. Glasenapp, *The Doctrine of Karman*, p. 3.

same way *karma* unites with the self.[17] One should be careful that this sort of union is not understood in the sense of some homogeneous mixture for then they would be inseperable. The separation of the self from the *karmic* particles can be achieved by drying them up with the heat of penance and atonement, which leaves the self unmixed, light and buoyant shining in its own pristine glory. Also, instead of understanding the union of *karma* and self as an intermingling, it should be understood in a metaphorical sense where *karmic* matter hides the omniscience of the self like a dense cover of clouds hinders sun light. So, the *karma* does not mix with the self as fire is absorbed in iron-ball or milk mixes with water. Rather, the correct understanding is to see *karma as* covering the essential qualities of the self like the cloud covers the brightness of the sun.[18] Further, this layer of *karma* on the self does not hinder or undermine the potential and the power of the self to attain its own nature. As when the light of the sun is veiled by clouds but there still remains some light, in same manner, *karma* can densify and obscure the true nature of the self but cannot destroy it.

Having explained the relation and the union between the material *karma* and the immaterial self, we have a fundamental question before us. Why is material *karma* at all attracted to the self to form a union and become bonded? Again, the pertinent reply comes forth in the form of an analogy. We very well know

17. Devendra Suri, *Karmagrantha*, Vol. 1, Agra: Shree Atmananda Pustak Mandal, 1918, p.2.

18. Chandranarayan Mishra, *The Problem of Nescience in Indian Philosophy*, Darbhanga: Mithila Institute of Post Graduate Studies and Research in Sanskrit Learning Series 3, 1977, p. 177.

that it is the nature of the magnet and the gravity of the Earth to attract or pull the iron particles and objects naturally. Also, just like a piece of cloth when put into a liquid absorbs it, in the same manner it is in the nature of the self to attract and stick *karma* particles on it. [19] Thus, it is the presence of the magnetism in the self which brings the influx of *karma* on to the self.

The activity of the mind, speech and body influenced by five senses, four passions, five indulgences (injury, lying, stealing, incontinence and possessiveness) and twenty five urges (clinging, promotion of deluded views, urge for gratifications, criminal activities, inventing weapons, urge to keep deluded world views, physical enthusiasm, etc.) are the doors (causes) for the inflow of *karma* in the form of both physical and psychical *karma*. [20] Evil activity brings about harmful *karmas* (demerit) and good actions bring about good *karma* (merit).

Both these *karma* bring upon results which obscure the true nature of self as well as determine the age, status, physique of the agent. Thus, *karma* is understood to be of eight main types in accordance with the duration of its fruition (*sthitī*), intensity of fruition (*anubhāga* or *rasa*), nature of fruition (*prakṛti*) and number of space-points (*pradeśas*).[21] These eight chief types of *karma* conceal the true nature of self and determine the physical existence of the

19. K.V. Mardia, *The Scientific Foundations of Jainism*, Delhi: Motilal Banarsidass, 1990, p. 16.
20. TS, 6.6, pp.152-3.
21. Glasenapp, *The Doctrine of Karman*, p.4.

agent. They are, knowledge-obscuring *karma* (*jñānāvarnīya karma*), perception-obscuring *karma* (*darśanāvarnīya karma*), feeling producing *karma* (*vedanīya karma*), deluding *karma* (*mohanīya karma)*, age determining *karma* (*āyuśa karma*), physique making *karma* (*nāma karma*), status determining *karma* (*gotra karma*), power obscuring *karma* (*antarāya karma)*.[22]

These eight main types of *karma* are characterised into two sub types viz., the obstructive (*ghāti-karma*) and the non-obstructive (*aghāti-karma*). The former create hindrance to the power of knowledge and intuition of the self taking it into wrong directions and obstructing its inherent energy. They are of four kinds namely: *jñānāvaranīya*, *darśnāvaranīya*, *mohanīya* and *antarāya*. Some of them are completely obscuring (*sarvaghātin*) and others are partially obscuring (*deśaghātin*). The latter do not obscure the essential nature of the self (*vedanīya-karma, nāma-karma, gotra-karma* and *āyuśa-karma)*. The destruction of the effects of *ghāti-karma* requires intense effort, whereas the results or effects of *aghāti-karma* can be destroyed easily. After the destruction of the four *ghāti-karma,* an individual self attains omniscience *(kevalin)* climbing the ladder of the fourteen *guṇasthānas,* but it cannot attain the final disembodiment or liberation (*mokṣa*) unless the four *aghāti-karma* are destroyed. To clarify this, attainment of omniscience does not mean the completion of the age determining (*āyuśa*) *karma.* One has to complete the given lifetime of the present existence. After completing it there is final release from the cycle of birth and death. This

22. *Ibid.*

means that the self becomes free and realised, established in its own nature *(siddha)* at the destruction of *karmas*.[23] It is further accepted by Jainas that the self does not lose all its essential characteristics even if it is infected by all obstructive *karma (sarvaghāti-karma)*. This has already been shown with the analogy of the sun and cloud.

The passions attracted by the self determine the intensity and duration of the *karmas*. If the strength of passions is strong, one will experience more evil deeds. In a similar manner, the intensity of bearing results of actions and duration of good *karma* correspond to the intensity of passions in the reverse order. In better words, the duration of the actions of immoral deeds is longer; the intense effects of the bad tendencies weaken the effect of the good deeds. The greater strength of character and conduct in a person reduces the duration and intensity of immoral deeds and promotes good tendencies.[24]

It is further explained that the intensity of the fruition of pleasure giving *karma (sātāvedanīyakarma)* is maximum because of pure intentions whereas the intensity of the fruition of pain giving *karma (asātāvedanīyakarma)* is maximum due to impure feelings.[25] The amount of *karmic* particles attracted by the self varies in accordance with the passion oriented activity of the self. If vibrations

---

23. K.Walli, *Theory of Karman*, Varanasi: Bharata Manisha Research Series 10, 1977, pp. 265-8.
24. Glasenapp, *The Doctrine of Karman*, p.27.
25. *Ibid.*, p. 74.

of the self are strong then it attracts more *karmic* particles. Low vibrations on the other hand, attract less *karmic* matter. Therefore, the self attracts *karmic* dirt through the vibrations created by unbelief (*mithyātva*), lack of self-discipline (*avirati*), activity (*yoga)* and passions (*kaśāya)*.[26] But this inflow can be stopped (*saṃvara*) and the acquired *karma* can be destroyed (*nirjarā*) by six ways: control (*gupti)*, careful movement (*samiti*), morality (*dharma*), reflection (*anuprekṣā*), conquering hardships (*parīṣaha*) and enlightened conduct (*cāritra*).[27] And finally one can attain total annihilation of the *karmas* which leaves the self emanicipated (*kaivalya*).

Thus, Jaina philosophy presents an elaborate account of *karma* such as is attracted by the self due to its vibrations and passions. This has also thrown light on the concept of the agent in Jaina view. Now we can move on to the relevant discussion of agency in Jainism.

II

For Jainas, the self (*jīva*) is the underlying, enduring, conscious entity of all the psychic events as well as actions. Unlike AdvaitaVedānta, in Jainism the words '*jīva*' and '*ātman*' are used synonymously. "...the *jīva* is the same as the *ātman* in the state of bondage and the *ātman* is the same as the *jīva* in the state of

---

26. *Ibid.*, p.74.
27. TS, 9.2, p. 219.

liberation"[28] Jaina tradition believes in the identity of doer and the experiencer. In *Dravyasaṃgraha*, Nemichandra defines *jīva*:

> as characterized by consciousness (*cetnā*) that is concomitant with sentience (*upayoga)*, perception (*darśana*) and knowledge (*jñāna*), is incorporeal (*amūrta*), a causal agent (*kartā*), coextensive with the body, enjoyer of the fruits of *karma* (*bhoktā*), having the world as its abode, emancipated (*siddha*), and of the nature of darting upward.[29]

Here, *upayoga* which can be understood as conscious attentiveness is of two kinds: intuition (*darśana*) and knowledge (*jñāna*).[30] Interestingly, one feature in which the Jaina conception of *jīva* is unique and makes it different from all other systems of Indian philosophy is its nature of '*ananta ātma-pradeśa*', i.e. the self when in embodiment occupies innumerable space points throughout the body of any *jīva*. This is the reason why the size of the self is akin to the body and it either expands or contracts according to the size of the body of the *jīva*.[31] Although in its purest state self or consciousness is formless and infinite but inthe state of bondage it appears to have dimension and finitude. So, the *jīva* is conceived as an eternal substance *(dravya)* of limited, but variable magnitude. It is thus capable of adjusting its size to the dimensions of physical body in which it happens to be housed for the time being. The light of lamp, for instance, can

---

28. P.T. Raju, *Structural Depths of Indian Thought*, New Delhi: South Asian Publishers, 1985, p.120.

29. *Dravyasaṃgraha* of Muni Nemichandra, (tr.) Sarat Chandra Ghoshak, Bombay: Shri Chandraprabha Digamber Jain Mandir Trust, 1986, p. 2.

30. Jagdish Prasad Jain, 'Jaina Psychology', *Handbook of Indian Psychology*, Delhi, India: Cambridge University Press, 2009, p.64.

31. Sinha, *Indian Philosophy*, p. 221.

occupy any kind of space. If the room is round, it occupies a round space; if it is rectangular, it occupies a rectangular space. If the room is small, it occupies a small space, and if big, a large space.[32] Similarly, as we have already mentioned the self can occupy the space of the body with which it is connected. In an ant, the self is as small as the ant; but in an elephant, it is as big. It is the nature of the self to become small or big until it becomes as large as the universe itself. Yet by nature it has no shape, but takes on the shape of the object with which it identifies itself.[33]

According to Jainism, an individual self who is the performer of actions is capable of attaining infinite knowledge. Knowledge/consciousness is the essential nature of the self but not an adventitious quality. The embodied self, when it comes in contact with mind (*manas*) as an instrument, leads to knowledge. But it is also the case that the *jīva* can know everything without the mind. The presence of mind functions only to limit the *jīva's* knowledge, and is necessary for the *jīva* in bondage, when the *jīva* cannot know the objects without mind and sense organs. The *jīva* is not merely the knower (*jñātā*) but also the enjoyer (*bhoktā*). Knowledge is conceived here as self-luminous (*svayaṁ-prakāśa*), so that it shows to the *jīva* not only the objects external to it but also itself. It pertains to the *jīva*, but not in the sense of an external possession. It is but a mode (*paryāya*) of the *jīva*. As mentioned above it is

32. TS, 5.16, p. 127.

33. Chainasukhdasa, *Jaina Darsana Sāra*, Jaipur: Veer Pustak House, 1980, pp. 9-12.

capable of modifying its size but can also undergo changes of form, retaining its size; and knowledge, which leads to the revelation of objects. The point is that the object known is regarded as existing outside and independently of the knowledge. As surely as there is a subject that knows, Jainism says, so surely is there an object that is known. Experience without something that is experienced is meaningless. For this reason, the doctrine is described as realistic. It is also pluralistic, since it believes in manifoldness of both self and matter.[34]

The nature of the self is to reveal itself and the objects in all acts of cognition. The conscious activity of the self constitutes in its psychic apparatus which facilitates all acts of cognition. This activity of the self is explained by J.P. Jain in the following way:

> When consciousness manifests itself in the psychic activity of apprehending or comprehending i.e. perceiving and cognizing of objects, it is called conscious attentiveness or cognition. When it reacts to the objects or situations with psychic dispositions of agreeable or disagreeable, likes and dislikes, it is described as feeling or emotion; and when it results in activity it takes the form of willing or conation. Individual self is thus, knower, enjoyer, or experiencer and active agent.[35]

But it is also capable of revealing the objects directly without the help of mind and the senses. Jainism recognizes two distinct kinds of knowledge, immediate *(aparokṣapratyakṣa)* and mediate *(parokṣa pratyakṣa)*. The bipartite classification of knowledge has therefore exclusive reference to the way in

---

34. *Ibid.*, pp. 4-5,12.

35. Jain, 'Jaina Psychology', p.61.

which objects are made known by the self. The fire, for example, that is inferred from observing smoke is known in a manner which is different from that in which a pot that is perceived is known. The former knowledge is mediate which includes various modes of knowing such as inference and verbal testimony, and the latter, whether classed as inference or perception, is immediate. Jainas do not regard even perception as immediate knowledge, because it is mediated by mind and senses. There is always the possibility of mistakes in the case of mediate knowledge, because mind and senses may go wrong. Immediate knowledge is obtained directly by the consciousness of the *ātman* itself. One who has perfect immediate knowledge can know anything in the world, however distant that object may be. But the self looses its power of omniscience through the impurities accumulated by action *(karma)* which enters it. The embodied self *(jīva)* is the substantive cause or the agent of the actions. The all-pervading conscious self becomes veiled and limited by its own *karma* (as has been explained in section I of this chapter). In order to regain the original omniscience, therefore agents must on their own get rid of *karma*, when an agent succeeds in getting rid of all actions and its impurities from individual self; there is attainment of omniscience *(Kaivalya)*. The knowledge thus obtained is without the mediation of instruments of knowledge like mind and senses. It is knowledge in its pristine form, and is termed primary perception *(mukhyapratyakṣa)*. It may be described as intuition, comprehending, as it does, all things and all phases of them.[36] In fact, *kevalajñāna* is described not merely as comprehending all things in their entirety but also as super-sensuous, unique and of inconceivable splendour *(apratyakṣa-vibhūti-viśeṣa)*.[37] The possessor of such knowledge is the worthy one (an *arham*) or the perfected (*siddha*), a conception which very much resembles that of the *jīvanmukta* in *Upaniṣadic* thought. Jainism emphasizes the importance of getting rid of *karma* to become a *Kevalin* or to become free from the circle of transmigration.[38] It is the activity of the self *(jīva)* that explains the influx of *karma* into the self. Therefore, we can say that the self is accepted as the agent (*kartā*) as well as the experiencer (*bhoktā*) of the fruits of actions done.

The agency of the self is clearly elucidated by Kundakundāchārya in his text *Samayasāra*. The self is said to be active, at least to some extent and modifiable by dispositions *(bhāvas)* suchas anger (*krodha*), greed (*lobha*) etc. *Bhāvas* are understood as the states of the self, which the self "makes" or "produces", presumably by a process of modification.[39] This modification can be known through the process of the application of consciousness called *upayoga*. Ignorance, intemperance and error when are of the nature of *jīva* are modes of

---

36. TS, 1.30, p. 22.

37. Pūjyapāda's commentary- '*Sarvārthasiddhi*', 10.1 (given in Tantia's translation of the *Tattvārtha Sūtra*), p. 253.

38. *Ibid.*, pp. 46-47.

39· SS, v.3.23.91

consciousness (*upayogarūpa*).[40] Indeed, they are modifications of *upayoga* connected with ignorance. The application of consciousness is in itself a *bhāva* that is pure and unsullied. Again, whatever further psychic states *(bhāva)* it creates, it is its agent.

The self can be connected with many psychic dispositions (*bhāva*s). The ignorant self due to erroneous knowledge produces ignorant dispositions *(bhāvas)*. In contrast knowledgeable self with right knowledge produces knowledgeable dispositions *(bhāvas)*.This can be further clarified by stating that the ignorant self itself is wrong knowledge and due to this wrong knowledge it is involved with *karma*. But self being aware of its true nature manifests itself through right knowledge and therefore, due to this right knowledge it does not entangle with any *karma*.[41] Thus, the individual self becomes agent and enjoyer under the sway of wrong knowledge.

Further clarified, from the empirical point of view, the self is said to be the agent of psychic disposition (*bhāva karma*) as well as the agent of material *karma* (*dravya karma*).[42] The relation between the *bhāva karma* and *dravya karma* is understood as follows: due to the arising of psychic dispositions *karmic* matter is attracted towards the self. In other words, from the practical point of view self is the agent of the material *karma*. But the same position,

40. SS, 3.20.88.

41. SS, 3.62.130.

42. SS, 3.23.91.

when understood from transcendental point of view, brings to light that the self is only the agent of its own psychic dispositions and not the agent of material *karma*. Further, this agency which is ascribed to the self is an outcome of the conditioning of the self with three impurities that are: erroneous faith, nescience and non-abstinence.[43] Also, whatever psychic dispositions are produced by the self, whether virtuous or its opposite; the self becomes the agent as well the experiencer of the resulting *karmas* of those dispositions.[44] Again, from the pure transcendental point of view, it is said by Kundakunda, that the self in its purity is not the agent of either the *bhāvakarma* or the *dravyakarma* but is only the experiencer of its own states.

At this point confusion is likely to enter: "Believing not self to be self, and self to be non-self, the ignorant soul becomes the causal agent of various *karma*."[45] The self thinks it becomes the agent of the *karma*s, but this is due to ignorance. In reality it is not. The self possessed of correct knowledge knows better: "The knowing self, who does not engender feelings of non-self as self, and self as non-self; that self does not become the causal agent of various karmas."[46] When the self realizes that its own nature is opposed to and distinct from what it is not (material or *achit*) then there comes an understanding that it is not the causal agent of *karma*s. The sense of agency subsides with the awareness of the truth

43. SS, 3.22.90.
44. SS, 3.34.102.
45. SS, 3.24.92.
46. SS, 3.25.93.

i.e the realisation of its infinite qualities. Kundakunda clarifies that "The self who does not engage in doing *karma*, such as knowledge-obscuring *karma*, which are consequences of the *karmic* matter, but only knows these *karmas*, is the knower."[47]

To sum up the above discussion we can say that there are two fundamentally different realms. One is of *karma*, which is the material substance, and the other is the self. The self, though not without activity, is not the agent of anything that takes place in the *karma* which belongs to the material realm. However, it can have a causal effect on *karma*, through its activity within its own realm. One can therefore say that the self produces *karma*, but only figuratively. In this context the quotation of Kundakunda from *Samayasāra* is relevant:

> The soul is perceived as an intrinsic agent for the modifications of the *karmic* bondages (knowledge obscuring *karma* etc.) and it is figuratively said that the *karma* has been produced by the soul. A war is fought by the warriors still it is figuratively said that the king is at war. Similarly, it is said from the empirical point of view, that the *jīva* or the soul has produced the *karma*.[48]

From the above analogy it becomes clear that there is a psycho-physical parallelism between the mind and its modification on the one hand, and the matter and its material modifications on the other. In this way the two series are interrelated and are running simultaneously parallel to each other. This implies that neither can matter become mind nor can mind become matter. The

47. SS, 3.33.101.

48. SS, 3.37.105-3.38.106.

individual self *(jīva)* is the agent of its own dispositions *(bhāvas)*, as it causes its own results. It is not the agent of material action *(pudgala-karmas)*. Also, the self remains an agent until it takes up the path of renunciation and atonement to burn off the *karmic* fetters.[49]

Thus, it is observed that in Jainism the empirical self *(jīva)* is the agent, doer, knower as well as the experiencer. The agent attracts different *karma* particles towards itself by way of mental, bodily and speech acts. But, from the transcendental point of view, *jīva* by overcoming all its passions and desires becomes an omniscient being *(Parmātman)*. It can, therefore, be said that the omniscient self by itself is neither the doer nor the experiencer of itself.

III

In this section we will expedite the concept of freedom of the agent (*jīva*). Christopher K. Chapple has written a very convincing informative paper on the conception of freedom in Jainism. I have relied on Chapple's framework and references but have added my own to arrive at my conclusion as well.[50] I will mention them in the course of my discussion. The scope of freedom is discussed in the sense of the power of agent to transcend the complex web of *karma* by the observance of five great vows *(pañcamahāvrata)*. According to Jainism, 'will' along with 'volition' is the foremost reason in the accumulation as well as

49. SS, 8.49.285

50. Christopher K.Chapple, 'Freewill and Voluntarism in Jainism', *Freewill, Agency and Selfhood*, (ed.) Bryant and Dasti, Oxford University Press, 2104, pp. 68-69.

the shrugging off of *karma*. Through the acts of will guided by evil tendencies and intent, *karma* is attracted to the self. Similarly, when the will is inspired by a desire not to do harm *karma* is shed off; leaving the self lighter and less burdened and ultimately free to raise high into endless energy, consciousness and bliss.[51] There is an acceptance of freewill on the part of an individual on account of the power and knowledge possessed by the person. Though one's life span, experience of pleasure and pain, and birth are determined by one's past *karmas,* the Jainas talk about all the opportunities and ways of transforming one's future for the better. An extreme insistence on the law of non-violence is to be observed in the minutest detail at the level of thought, word and deed and this distinguishes Jainism from other schools of thought. It is the understanding of non-violence which helps one to elevate and possess more control in the form of power to restrain all the vices. This enhances one's operational freedom to do good deeds and refrain from doing evil acts thus creating one's own future well-being.

The *Ācārāṅga Sūtra* (AS) one of the oldest text of Jaina tradition has laid down rules of observances with regard to performance and prohibition of action for the people who have taken the ascetic vow and also for lay practitioners. It invokes adherence to the five great vows as the primary way of remaining steadfast on the path to attaining freedom from bondage. The opening passage clearly defines the realistic understanding of the wordly existence as "believes

51. *Ibid.*

in the self, believes in the world, believes in reward, and believes in action. In the world, these are all the causes of sin which must be comprehended and renounced."[52] The Jaina tradition lays great emphasis on the careful handling of volitional activity. It is clarified that extreme care should be taken while doing actions so that they do not lead to violence in any form, whether at the level of thoughts, words or deeds. One should willingly refrain from doing harm nor tell others to do harm, nor endorse or participate with someone involved in doing the harm.[53] According to Chapple, a voluntarist[54] view of the 'will' is propagated in *Āchārāṇga Sūtra*. It starts with the acknowledgement of the presence of life in its most basic forms and then looks for its presence in more complex organisms such as bacteria, plants and animals etc. Since in Jainism observance of non-violence is uncompromisable, therefore it is absolutely mandatory for Jaina monastics to be vigilant in their activity so that they do not commit any injury to all forms of life. This observance has to be practiced from the minutest level for the minutest living beings, be it one, two, three, four or five sensed. It also explains that one can experience severe punishments in the present life due to actions done in past life i.e there is a relation between the moral quality of one's actions which bring results in the form of pleasure or pain one has to undergo in other births. The existence of various health

52. AS, p. 44.

53. Chapple, 'Freewill and Voluntarism', p. 70.

54. This term is used by Chapple for Jaina understanding of freedom where an individual is self-governed having an exercising control over the 'will'. I also feel convinced to this usage of the term and hence have utilized it for Jaina explication of freedom of action.

problems such as "boils, leprosy, consumption, falling sick, blindness and stiffness, lameness and humpbackedness, dropsy and dumbness, epilepsy, eye disease etc, to the fruits of their own acts"[55] are accepted as the result of the performance of bad actions. Detailed rules are given governing the life of laity as well as monks and nuns to get rid of all the afflictions that causes unpleasant experiences. Thus, in *Achārāṇga Sūtra*, one finds not only a philosophy and way of life based on voluntary action, but also exhaustive and somewhat detailed prescription and proscription for one's behaviour. It has been insisted that one is ethically responsible for any sort of action being done by a person whether intentionally or unintentionally. One's exercise of freedom consists in not surrendering to passions and desires by adopting the ethical values and moral principles.

In the *Tattvārtha Sūtra* (TS)[56] of Umāsvāti, we can gather from discussions a deep-seated commitment to freewill. It begins with the declaration that right world view, right knowledge and right conduct are the pathways which lead to liberation.[57] Then it goes on to explain the journey of the souls from one level of existence to the other based on their acquisition of *karmas*. It explains the working hierarchy of the different states of existence in different spheres that beings travel into finally leading to liberation *(kevalajñāna)*. It contrasts self

55. Chapple, 'Freewill and Voluntarism', p.71.

56. TS, pp. 5-11.

57. TS, 1.1, p.5.

with matter, the influx and binding of *karma* with the stoppage and expulsion of *karma*. Each self authors its own future existence, inviting *karma* to stick to and obstruct its true nature or actively expelling *karma* through the performance of purifying vows.[58] According to Umāsvāti, the association of the self and matter is beginningless. The Jaina belief that *karma* flows onto the self, sticks to it and shrouds it with tendencies and predispositions are reconfirmed. Through the voluntary taking up of religious life or the ethical path, one is able to stop the influx of more *karma* and then gradually slough off the *karma* that have accrued over past. Each self creates and follows a solitary destiny. Vows must be observed and performed from within; no human being and no god or demon can affect either adherence to or straying from commitment to expel all the fetters of *karma*. The text delineates the cosmological order consisting of three domains of existence: the infernal region, the middle realm of earth and the heavenly region.[59] It describes the lower and middle region, comprising a remarkable geography interwoven with moral implications. If one performs evil actions, one descends into various hells. Likewise if one does benevolent actions, one ascends into heaven. Various islands have been talked about within the middle region. One of them is *Jambudvīpa* consisting of seven continents, mountains, lakes etc. where elements, plants, human as well as non-human animals exist. Within these only on three continents of Bharata, Airāvata and

58. TS, 1.4, p. 6.

59. TS, Chapter 3 and 4 contain these discussions.

Videha spiritual effort is possible for human beings who are given the opportunity to cultivate virtue.[60] Utmost importance is given to birth in the realm of human beings as even if one has attained heaven one still cannot attain liberation until and unless one takes birth as a human being and strives for liberation.

The *Tattvārtha Sūtra* explains five major vows as already mentioned[61] which are further supplemented with seven minor vows namely:

> refraining from movement beyond a limited area, restricting movement to an even more limited area, refraining from wanton destruction of the environment by thought, word or deed, keeping aloof from sinful conduct for a set period of time, fasting on sacred days and observing restrictions at secluded places, limiting the use of consumable and non-consumable goods, offering alms to wandering ascetics.[62]

And these vows ultimately culminate in the act of the Jaina 'will' i.e the vow to gradually fast till death. But this should be free from any desires for the results or rewards of fasting and one should accept it with joy and right mindedness without any impulsiveness.[63] Just as volitional *karma* delivers individual selves into repeated births in the infernal, elemental, microbial, plant, animal, human and heavenly realms, the practice of vows reverses this process.[64] It is also advocated that the moral behaviour is the key to spiritual progression along the

60. TS, 3.16, p.86
61. TS 7.1
62. TS 7.16, p.177
63. TS, 7.17, p.178
64. TS, 7.1, p. 169

fourteen stages (*guṇasthānas*) that lead to freedom.[65] The text defines morality as "perfect forgiveness, humility, straightforwardness, purity, truthfulness, self-restraint, austerity, renunciation, detachment and continence."[66] The will is required to adhere to the vows and to overcome the influence of past *karmas*. No external influences play the role for the determination of the will to accept ethical path of life. There is sheer self-determinism resulting in volitional adoption of any vow. All of this effort finds its momentum when there is no fresh bondage because the causes of bondage have been eliminated and all destructive *karmas* have worn off. Within this moment of freedom, the efforts of all spiritual exertion have borne fruit, delivering the self forever from the cycle of rebirth.

The *Tattvārtha Sūtra* can be seen as a practical guide to transform one's character to transform oneself and attain higher states of consciousness (perfect knowledge). It asserts that human action determines the nature of how one feels about the world one occupies. *Karma* theory in this text has no external agency. Jaina *tīrthaṇkars* like Mahāvīra and Parśvanātha can be seen as the exemplars of inspiration and guide posts for reforming one's life and actions but they cannot intervene to create or alter others *karma*. Each individual is solely responsible for one's own *karma* having the ingenious power to alter the course of their lives whether in right direction or otherwise.

---

65. TS, 9.5, p. 220

66. TS, 9.6, p. 221

Chapple has also discussed Kundakundācharya's take on non-attachment of the self to attain liberation. I will try to build my discussion only concentrating on Kundakunda's *Samaysāra*. In this work he explicates about 'the self-governed nature of the Self'. It highlights that the self though burdened with the *karmic* matter has complete autonomy to realise its freedom. The text explores in every aspect as to what the nature of self is from what it is not. With the help of analogies clear distinctions are made to understand the nature of ignorance, so that one seperates itself from what it is not. This Kundakunda explains using the Jaina method of relative judgement invoking the two standpoints from which the reality can be understood. They are empirical standpoint (*vyavāhara naya*) and the transcendental standpoint (*niścaya naya*).

Kundakunda repeatedly says that the self has to attain the discriminative knowledge which indicates that the self in itself is capable as well as to an extent free to pursue its path for knowing its own self. Though he does not get into the detailed discussion of the means of doing that in *Samayasāra,* he keeps on emphasizing that when discriminative knowledge enlightens the performance of actions, the agent stops the influx of *karma.*[67] The self on its own with its inherent powers guards itself from the performance of both good and bad deeds which in turn brings about merit and demerit. It is the continuous awareness of the self of its infinite characteristics which keeps it detached from any sort of external influences where internal influences (passions etc.) have already been

67. SS, 6.3.183.

won over by it. This sort of establishment of the self in its own nature purges it from all the baggage of *karma* to elevate it to the status of a pure self *(Parmātman)*.[68]

The one whose perception is purified by right belief experiences the results of the previously performed actions without attachment as the witness and knower (*jñātā* and *dṛṣṭā* respectively).[69] This leads to the shedding of *karma* as well as stops the fresh inflow of *karma*. For e.g. an expert on toxicology is able to handle poison without getting affected by it, in the same way the right knower enjoys/ experiences the arising of the fruits of the *karmas*.[70]

Also, the right believer (who has overcome attachments), when involved in any sensual activity does not indulge into it. The way an assistant performs all duties on behalf of the businessman but does not become the owner of it, so, a right believer remains non-indulgent due to absence of attachments, whereas the wrong believer remains indulgent.[71]

The Omniscient masters (*kevalajñāni*) have described the various outcomes of the fruition of *karmas* but none of them are of the nature of self. The self is the only knower *(jñātā)*.[72] In the presence of material and psychical *karmas* along with the changing dispositions *(bhāvas)* the self cannot know its real

68. SS, 6.7.187-6.9.189.

69. SS, 7.1.193-7.2.194.

70. SS, 7.3.195

71. SS, 7.5.197

72. SS, 7.6.198

nature. So, one should leave or overcome such dispositions and should become a conscious knower with stability.[73] The knowledge possessed by a knower is inclusive of five types of knowledge. They are: sensory knowledge (*matijñāna)*, scriptural knowledge (*śrutijñāna),* clairvoyance (*avadhijñāna),* telepathy (*manaḥparyāya*) and omniscience (*kevalajñāna*). All these together fulfil the acquisition of right knowledge which leads to liberation. All these above clarifications have been given by Kundakunda in order to induce detachment on the part of the agent (*jīva*) for it is said that "effort without right knowledge is useless."[74] Without getting into the complexities of the right action, how it is to be done and what actions are to be done and what avoided, Kundakunda focuses on the realisation or attainment of right knowledge which purifies all activities. He attempts to give a psychological understanding and route to overcome this bondage. But ultimately the will or intention to follow the vows and attachment to their rightness must also be abandoned. The very disposition to do something or not to do something results in bondage, whether that disposition gets translated into action or not. This is the crux of the cause of bondage from the transcendental point of view (*niścaya naya*). Similarly, five indulgences bring bondage and stopping those indulgences brings release.[75]

73. SS, 7.11.203.

74. SS, 7.12.204-7.13.205.

75. SS, 8.27.263-8.28.264.

"The understanding of the scriptures (*Āchārāṇga Sūtra*) is knowledge, (belief in) substances like *jīva* is faith, and (protection of six kinds of organisms) is conduct, this is the empirical point of view (*vyavahāra naya*)".[76] This practical standpoint of knowledge is contrasted with the transcendental standpoint of the same. Kundakunda says "surely the self is knowledge, the self is faith and conduct, the self is renunciation, and the self is stoppage of *karma* and *yoga;* this is the transcendental point of view (*niśćaya naya*)".[77]

The self and the *karmic* bondage are differentiated on the basis of their own inherent nature. These are separated with the help of instrument of self-discrimination. Through this one can separate the self from *karmic* bondage and realise the pure self as the seer and knower.[78] Then the agency of the individual self ceases to be.

From what has been discussed above we conclude that this text attempts to bring the discriminative knowledge for a seeker (*jīva*). Thus, all the misconceptions which are the result of ignorance, desires and passions have been said to be identified and known with self effort. This distinctly leads to the perception of the nature of the self in its pure state.

---

76. SS, 8.40.276
77. SS, 8.41.277
78. SS, 9.7.294-9.12.299

Thus, in summing up the Jaina view of freedom for action I bring in Chapple's words: "a thorough voluntarist outlook proclaiming that each individual carries ultimate control over his or her own life. *Karma* determines all things, and each self faces, moment to moment, the decision to continue in patterns of behaviour that densify *karma* and hence obscure the self or take up the steady path to purification." [79] I am in agreement with Chapple's conception of freedom because here persons have autonomy and are self-governed to conduct their 'will' in accordance with the ethical path laid down by the masters. Also, this gives us an understanding that even though one's passionate influences play a vital role in one's conduct i.e. actions may be determined and can be the outcome of these even then the self with the power of conscience (*upayoga*) can positively modify these tendencies and overcome them. This brings the purity of character, action and knowledge. In this sense, we can say that Jaina thought accept a compatibilist sense of freedom. Here, the agent is not coerced from outside into making choices but is determined by their own will and at the same time is free to choose their actions. Also, there is always a possibility of making a better choice of action in ethical terms at the instance of choosing. In this sense Jainism can be said to support both the senses of compatibilism, i.e., one determines one's actions freely without any external influences as well as has the 'freedom to choose' another action at the time of making one's choice had they so wanted (mentioned in the introduction on pp.12-14). Thus, it can be

79. Chapple, 'Freewill and Voluntarism', p. 84.

said that Jainas accept determinism but their understanding of it does not go to the extreme of fatalism. They can be said to accept the voluntarist model of compatibilism. According to their world view an agent seeks to attain 'freedom from' the *karmic* bondage by stopping the influx of *karma* into soul and for so doing one is freely determined by one's own will to achieve the true nature of the self. This is 'freedom to'.

In the conclusion, we can reiterate that freedom has to be gained from *karmic* bondage ('freedom from'). We can affirm that in Jainism liberation (*kaivalya*) comes through the separation of self with its *karmic* impurities by recourse to attaining right or perfect perception, knowledge and conduct (*triratna*). This path further demarcates in ethical terms a resolution for tolerance for all forms of life, an ascetic way of life, absolute moral behaviour and meditative contemplation, abandoning the mistaken distinction between oneself and others. In Jainism, extreme insistence on non-violence by way of thought, word and deed leads to uncompromising care and no harm to all forms of life including miniscule organisms. Though from the ultimate point of view (*niścaya naya)* the self is not the agent but from the empirical point of view (*vyavahāra naya*) it is the doer of both psychical and material *karmas*. The agency of the individual self (*jīva*) culminates in the realisation of its power where action in the form of exertion and effort is indispensable to remove the *karmic* fetters, which in turn frees the soul from its entanglement, eventually leading to even the cessation of the sense of agenthood/doership. Finally, it can be said that Jaina philosophy upholds a path of movement of the self (*jīva*) from an impure state (ignorant and violent) to a state of unconditioned purity (knowledge and non-violence). And in this journey the *jīva* is the lone agent, who has to with its own effort, achieve liberation.

III

Karma, Agency and Freedom in Early Buddhism

Buddhism as an independent tradition originated around the 6th century BC in ancient India.[1] It was originally a part of the *Samana* tradition, which gave rise to various schools of thought including Cārvāka, Jainism etc. The founder of this school was Siddhārtha Gautama, better known as The Buddha (the enlightened one). Buddhism later developed into various sects with the emergence of new thoughts and ideas. However, the basic beliefs remained the same and are common between all the later sects of Buddhism. These are briefly enunciated: Buddha believed that a person's curiosity for addressing perennial questions on God, soul, universe, heaven etc. would not lead him to address his immediate malady: suffering or *dukkha*. Thus, the focus must be on getting over suffering and striving for salvation, for it alone brings peace and release. With this approach, he delivered his four Noble Truths (*Ariya Sacca*): There is suffering or misery (*dukkha*), suffering has a source or cause (*dukkhasamudaya)*, suffering can be removed (*dukkhanirodha*), There is a path (Eight-fold Path) for the removal of suffering (*dukkhanirodhamagga*).

There are certain doctrines which are hidden within these four Noble Truths and can be expressed below:

1. The term 'Buddhism' in this dissertation refers specifically to 'Early Buddhism' .

It is a fact of human life that anyone who takes birth is liable to undergo pleasant and unpleasant experiences. Sickness, old age and finally death are harsh realities of life. Although we witness these unpleasant experiences in us or others, nonetheless we tend to overlook their reality and avoid facing them. Desire for permanence brings discontent, disharmony, imperfection, physical and mental suffering.[2]

The second noble truth highlights the doctrine of causation (*paṭiccasamuppāda)*. This perennial existence of suffering is not without any cause. The reality of impermanence (the world of change) when taken to be permanent/ unchanging, becomes the cause of suffering. Buddha maintained that any existent being is dependent on something else for its existence. This dependency is possible because these beings are seen as aggregates. Since everything is dependent there is a constant flow of birth, decay and death. In other words, there is no permanence that can be found. Hence, the doctrine of impermanence was preached by the Buddha.

Everything being impermanent shows that even causes and their effects are changeable. Buddha showed a way out from this chain of cause (ignorance) and effect (suffering) through his third noble truth. He asserted that suffering can be stopped. The root cause of suffering is ignorance, and ignorance leads to desire, attachment and craving. This in turn leads to suffering. The moment it is

2. Bina Gupta, *An Introduction to Indian Philosophy: Perspectives on Reality, Knowledge and Freedom*, New York and London: Routledge, 2012, p.82.

gone, with the knowledge and realisation of the Noble Truths, suffering disappears as well. For example, the flame of a lamp keeps burning till the time it is connected with the oil and the wick and doesnot go off till the time these conditions remain steady. Similarly, these three obstructions (desire, attachment and craving) are connected to ignorance and in turn lead to clinging (*upādāna*) which then leads to thirst *(tanhā)* for attainment of enjoyment. This continues to produce suffering unless the source of its occurrence i.e. ignorance is removed.[3]

And finally the last Noble Truth emphasizes on the action that is to be done for the cessation of suffering and the attainment of peace or nibbāna with the knowledge and realisation of all the noble truths. Buddha taught that *sīla* (right speech, right action and right living), *samādhi* (right effort, right mindfulness and right concentration) and *paññā* (right views and right resolve) must be cultivated simultaneously to attain the cessation of suffering.

Buddha's teachings were oral not recorded immediately and were orally transmitted through memorization. They were later recorded by his disciples through the years in what came to be known as the *Pāli* canon. This comprises of the *Tipiṭakas* namely: *Vinaya Piṭaka* (which contains the textual framework for the well being of the monastic community in terms of conduct that has to be followed by the monks and nuns), *Sutta Piṭaka* (which contains mainly a large number of discourses between the Buddha and his disciples and is of significant

3. G.P. Malalasekera, 'The Individual in Therāvāda Buddhism', *Philosophy East and West*, Vol. 14 (2), Hawaii: Hawaii University Press, 1964, p. 149.

philosophical importance) and *Abhidhamma Piṭaka* (which contains the systematic philosophical doctrines and principles underlying the nature of man and matter). In order to make my objective successful which is to bring out and analyse the relation between action *(kamma)*, its doer/agent and the latter's freedom to act, I will be referring to selections from the five *Nikāyas* contained in the *Sutta Piṭaka* namely: *Dīgha Nikāya* (DM), *Majjhima Nikāya* (MN), *Saṁyutta Nikāya* (SN), *Aṇguttara Nikāya* (AN) and *Khuddaka Nikāya* (KN).[4]

From what has been explained in the above introduction it emerges clearly that the role of the agent and his or her actions plays a significant role in the attainment of ultimate release or *nibbāna* which is the highest goal of human life according to Buddha. Henceforth this chapter aims to explore in detail the nature of the doer and that of the actions and the possibility here of the freedom to act, if any, according to Buddha.

I

Beginning with the conception of *kamma* from the early Buddhist point of view, it can be understood that whenever a person or an agent performs an action, the intention (*cetnā*) of doing that action determines the qualitative consequences that action will ensue. In *Nibbedhika Sutta*, Buddha remarks "intention, I tell you is *kamma*. Intending, one does *kamma* by way of body, speech and

4. I have only referrd to *Dhammapada* of *Khuddaka Nikāya*. Also, since the *Nikāyas* were written in Pāli, I have used Pāli terms instead of Sanskrit in this chapter.

intellect."[5] Thus, actions are accepted as mental, bodily and vocal. All the three have their origin in intention. As the determination is the intention, it is intention that determines the action. The nature of the intention rather than the outward appearance of the action determine the consequences that will ensue from action. So, if one appears to be benevolent but acts with greed, anger, hatred, etc. then the fruit of those actions will bear testimony to the fundamental intention that lay behind them (greed or hatred) and will become the cause for future experience of suffering and unhappiness.[6] The quality of intention along with the moral quality of the action determines the results actions will bring about. This is the reason why Buddha has laid great emphasis on intention behind the performance of actions and believes that it is intention which strongly determines the future states of existence. In support of this McDermott writes "...the Buddha came to recognize that beings pass from existence in accordance with the nature of their deeds (*kamma*)."[7]

The Buddha realised that the realm into which one is born is an outcome of the results of one's actions. In the *Majjhima Nikāya* it is said: "Thus with divine, purified, superhuman eye he sees beings passing away and being reborn. He knows that beings are inferior, exalted, beautiful, ugly, well-faring, ill-faring

5. AN, 6.63.
6. *Ibid.*, 5.57, *Upajjhatthana Sutta.*
7. James McDermott, 'Karma and Rebirth in Early Buddhism' in *Karma and Rebirth in Classical Indian Traditions*, Delhi: Motilal Banarsidass, 1983, p. 165.

according to (the consequences of) their *kamma*."[8] Human beings are always said to be the inheritors of their actions (*kamma*) and the results of those actions. Therefore, when Buddha saw beings passing from their present existence in accordance with their *kamma,* he is quoted as saying:

> These worthy beings who were well-conducted in body, speech, and mind, not revilers of noble ones, right in their views, giving effect to right views in their actions, on the dissolution of the body, after death, have reappeared in a happy destination, even in the heavenly world... have reappeared among human beings. But these worthy beings who were ill-conducted in body, speech, and mind, revilers of noble ones, wrong in their views, giving effect to wrong views in their actions, on the dissolution of the body, after death, have reappeared in the realm of ghosts... have reappeared in the animal world. Or these worthy beings who were ill conducted... have reappeared in a state of deprivation, in an unhappy destination, in perdition, even in hell.[9]

Buddha made it very clear that as are one's deeds, so are the future states of existence. Individuals take birth into different realms (*gati*) like: heaven, hell, human world, animal world etc. depending on the quality of their actions in terms of merit or demerit. *Kamma* as a causal factor not only conditions the birth of an individual in a particular realm but also accounts for the differences within that realm of beings like status, appearance, life span etc. This principle envisaged the inevitability of experiencing the results of one's past deeds. The results of the actions have to be borne in the present life and in some future existences. Through this principle Buddha also explained the inequality which exists in the world around us. One becomes what one is, not through birth, but

8. MN, 1.4.29, p. 106.

9. *Ibid.*p.106, *Bhayabherava Sutta*.

somewhat because of one's past acts. Birth and rebirth are the effects of *kamma*. This relation of cause (*kamma*) with its effect (*vipāka)* has been beautifully explained by Buddha in the second Noble Truth, with the theory of conditioned or dependent arising (*paṭiccasamuppāda)* where each factor in the cycle of birth and death determines the next factor in the chain.

Ignorance (*avijjā*)— Impressions (*saṅkhāra*)— Initial consciousness of the embryo (*viññāna*)—Mind and body, the embryonic organism (*nāma-rūpa*)—Six organs of knowledge (*saḍāyatana*)—Sense contact (*phassa*)—Sense experience (*vedanā)*—Thirst (*tanḥā)*— Clinging (*upādāna*)— Tendency to be born (*bhava*)— Rebirth (*jāti*)— Old age, death etc. (*jarā-maraṇam*).[10]

This sort of conditioned arising explains how intention conditions future existence but Buddha warns that one should not take it as an extreme view that one is either absolutely determined or absolutely free. Absolute determination will wipe off the possibility of following ethical path and reforming one's deeds and intention. So, total determinism cannot be accepted. Similarly, absolute freedom too wipes off the performance of ethical actions as then one will not be motivated to do good actions in the absence of any determining factors.

Although the Buddha strictly maintained a corresponding relation between the performance of the action and the consequences that arise from that action but in

---

10. Chatterjee and Datta, *An Introduction to Indian Philosophy,* Calcutta: Calcutta University Press, 2008, p. 120.

worldly states of affairs we may sometimes not see this direct correspondence. Thus, many times it is the case that a good deed performed brings immediate bad consequences in the form of pain or suffering, and vice-versa. This apparent paradox is resolved when one looks at the broader framework where the operations of *kamma* are not related to one birth but to many or all the previous births that an individual has undergone. The Buddha in fact gave answers to various questions to specific people in specific contexts, and it is possible to find several causal explanations of behaviour in the early Buddhist texts.

The pleasurable and painful experiences that an individual has to undergo owe their origin to the good or bad deeds performed by that individual only. When one is so conditioned by one's *kammas* then the obvious question arises: what constitutes 'good' deeds and 'bad' deeds? This can be answered by focussing on the *karmic* intentions which can be characterised as either wholesome (*kusala*) or unwholesome (*akusala*). Unwholesome deeds guided by the forces of greed (*lobha*), hatred (*dosa*) and delusion (*moha*) leads to de-meritorious actions which are killing, stealing, adultery, lying, slandering, covetousness, ill will and false belief. Whereas wholesome deeds are the outcome of the practice of morality *(pañcasikkhapada),* meditation *(samādhi) and* wisdom *(paññā)* leading to good actions like abstention from killing, stealing, sexual misconduct, false speech and covetousness.[11]

11. *Ibid.*, 8.39.; Steven Collins, *Selfless Persons,* Cambridge: Cambridge University Press, 1982, p. 90.

In the Buddhist theory of *kamma*, the *kammic* effects of a deed are not determined solely by the deed itself, but also by the general disposition of the person who commits the deed. This can be supported from what follows: In the *Acinteyya Sutta* it is said:

> Acertain person has not properly cultivated his body, behaviour, thought and intelligence, is inferior and insignificant and his life is short and miserable; of such a person... even a trifling evil action done leads him to hell. In the case of a person who has proper culture of the body, thought and intelligence, who is superior and not insignificant, and who is endowed with long life, the consequences of a similar evil action are to be experienced in this very life, and sometimes may not appear at all.[12]

Thus, a generally good person would suffer less for a deed than one who commits the same deed but is generally evil. It is also being said that the knowledge of how *kamma* of a person matures is one of the four incomprehensible which only an individual with an insight of a Buddha can see.[13]

Although each agent is inheritor of their own deeds alone, the maturation of *kamma* has consequences which reach beyond their self. In any given situation the *kamma* of all the individuals involved has to be in conjunction with that of every other participant in that situation. This has been discussed by McDermott with the help of an example:

> a fratricide could only be born of parents who because of their past *kamma* deserved the suffering that results from the violent loss of a child, who in turn deserved to suffer such a death at the hands of

12. AN, 1.249.

13. *Ibid.*, 2.80.

> his brother as punishment for his own past deeds. It is a matter not simply of the *kamma* of the one son leading to his own death, but of the confluence of the *kamma* of both the parents with that of both their sons. It is only in this sense of the confluence of the individual *kammic* reward and punishment of those involved in a given situation that it is possible to speak of 'group *kamma*' in the classical *Pāli* texts.[14]

Again, all pleasure, pain, and mental states that men experience need not be due to previous actions but could be due to bodily states of the doer. In answer to a question raised by Moliya Sivaka, Buddha replied that in addition to the effect of *kamma*, "certain experiences.... arise here originating from bile,... from phlegm,.... from wind,... resulting from the humours of the body,...born of the changes of the seasons,... of being attacked by advisers,... of spasmodic attacks."[15] Yet where deeds are performed intentionally, their fruition in time is inevitable. It is impossible that *kamma* should not work itself out as it is not the case that the mortal should not die. No human, super human or devil can escape the fruits of their actions. The action done by any individual determines the dispositions or the tendencies a person will carry to the future births i.e. they are the determinants which condition a person from within. Further, they also determine the circumstances that one will get around oneself i.e. the moral quality of the actions performed influence the good/happy or the bad/painful experiences that a person will go through in his/her life. There is an invariable relation between the qualities of the action performed and the rewards or

14. McDermott, 'Karma and Rebirth in Early Buddhism', p. 175.

15. SN,4.36.21, *Shivaka Sutta*.

punishment one gets. However, it is not necessary that any action performed will immediately start giving its results or will not give results. There can be any combination for the fruition of the results of the actions. The competing interplay of the *kammic* residues and tendencies are both robust and weak in intensity and they mature according to the supply of the conditions of their arising. Buddha rebutts the view that anybody who kills, lies, steals, and so forth will take rebirth in undesirable states.[16] He rather held that crooked or evil minded people may take birth into good place and circumstances. The same *Sutta* goes on to explain how we can bring together the inevitable working out of the effects of *kamma* with the beliefthat one gets what one does. Persons capable of doing good and evil actions get fruits of their results in either present existence or some future lifetimes. McDermott puts this relation aptly:

> Thus the effect of a comparatively weak deed may be superseded by the effect of a comparatively strong deed or by the accumulated effects of a series of deeds. This means that although an individual may have been a murderer, a liar and so forth, on death he may nonetheless arise in a pleasant state if the effects of his accumulated good deeds are sufficient to supersede the results of his wrong doing. The fruits of the deeds which have thus been superseded will then be experienced once the fruits of the deeds which have superseded them have been exhausted.[17]

It is in this sense that there are four sets of actions talked of by Buddha and is expressed as:

---

16. MN, 136, *Mahākammvibhaṇga Sutta*.

17. McDermott, 'Karma and Rebirth in Early Buddhism', p. 176.

> Thus, Ānanda, there is action that is incapable [of good result] and appears incapable; there is action that is incapable [of good result] and appears capable; there is action that is capable [of good result] and appears capable; and there is action that is capable [of good result] and appears incapable.[18]

As is the intensity of the residue of *kamma (vāsanā)* so will be its fruition determined in time.

Coming back to the intentional nature of *kamma* (mentioned earlier), to Buddha *kamma* is volition and what is born of volition, i.e. what a person does after having willed mentally, bodily or vocally. It may be further explained that if a man goes to a forest with an intention to kill animals, but does not succeed then his misconduct is not a bodily one. If he gives consent for doing a similar deed but is not actually carried out by the body then this will be a wrong deed of the speech and not of the body. The very intention of doing harm whether materialized into effect or not would still be a *kamma* of the mind.[19] In the absence of mental *kamma* no bodily or speech *kamma* can arise, as in the case of a realised one who is free of any intentional *kamma*.[20]

Thus, there can be no action without the mental act of willing it. For this reason it is being said that 'we are what we think, we are what we will'. No action can create a reserve for future retribution unless it is intentional and deliberate.

---

18. MN, 3.215, *Mahakammavibhanga Sutta*.

19. Surendranath Dasgupta, *A History of Indian Philosophy,* Vol.1, Delhi: Motilal Banarsidass, 1975, 2010, p.108.

20. MN, 3.212-213.

Intention *(cetnā),* the mental act leaves traces in the chain of thoughts which may further causally determine the future tendencies as well as actions. This becomes a part of the series of mental existence that takes the place of the self in Buddhism.

Thus, agent in Buddhism has to bear the fruits of actions he or she commits without fail. Intention (good or bad) determines the moral quality of any action which in turn creates various tendencies in the doers. This implies that doers are invariably linked to the results of the deeds performed by them which in turn makes them responsible for the same.

II

If one has to understand the sense in which human beings are considered inheritor of their *kamma*, and their travel from one existence to another then one should understand the nature of the agent according to early Buddhism. The agent is said to be a psycho-physical organism in Buddhism. Is this agent a person at all? Buddha taught the doctrine of impermanence, which implies that there is no enduring entity (self) which can be said to be transmigrating to the next birth. Even so then who is the agent as a psychological, non-enduring entity? How do we talk of responsibility in such a situation? For, no one can be held responsible unless there is an agent that has done the action voluntarily and intentionally. The metaphysical problem of no self (*anattā*) i.e. no abiding, underlying spiritual substance, makes it much more difficult to understand the relation between the action and its results. What or who is it then to which agency or doership is ascribed in Buddhism?

An agent is an empirical being or a human person who performs actions. To suppose or believe that this outward action is manifestation of some inner conscious enduring entity's activity was not acceptable to Buddha. He moved away from the extremes of accepting anything permanent (self) or accepting human person as only a physical body. Instead of propounding any absolute theory of human person, he analysed the various possibilities that were being attributed to it by his contemporaries[21] and analytically rejected their attribution. But this does not mean that Buddha did not say anything about 'who' the agent was?

He accepted that there is a performer of actions or the agent. In *Attakārī Sutta,* the Buddha rejects the view of no self-doer and the other-doer.[22] When a Brahmin approached Buddha with his acceptance of the view of 'there is no self-doer, there is no other-doer.'[23] Buddha rejected his view by saying that

> how indeed could one moving forward by himself, moving back by himself say: there is no self-doer, there is no other-doer? What do you think, Brahman, is there an element or principle to initiating or beginning an action?[24]

21. Spiritualists and Materialists.

22. AN, 3.337-338.

23. *Ibid.*

24. *Ibid.*

Although the Buddha taught that there is no permanent, eternal, changeless, independently existing self *(attā)*, he also taught that there is action and doing, and that it is therefore meaningful to speak of one who intends, initiates, sustains and completes actions and deeds, who is therefore an ethically responsible being. He also explains that there is a natural condition of beginning or undertaking action *(ārabbhadhātu)*[25] in the human beings or agents. This is how we clearly see the initiation of actions in ourselves and others. The agents in question are volitional beings capable of intentional activity as well as conscious effort.

These agents or human persons are explained by the Buddha most commonly and assertively with the Doctrine of Aggregates *(khandha)* and the Theory of Twelve Factors (*Dvādasangha*).

According to the doctrine of aggregates, a person is made of five aggregates or *khandhas*. These are *nāma* and *rūpa*. This further consists of material body (*rūpa*), feelings *(vedanā)*, perception (*saññā*), predispositions (*saṇkhāra*), and consciousness (*viññāna*). At any point of time a person is but a temporary combination of these aggregates. All the *khandhas* are subject to continuous change, transformation and destruction. The Buddha explained that one, who thinks that behind the aggregate there is a self which is the substratum of all the five *khandhas*, is mistaken. This is not so. One forms one's conception of the

25. *Ibid.*

self due to the formation of identity. Those who do not know the doctrine of impermanence become prey to such acceptance and regard "form as self,... feeling as self... perception as self... volitional formation as self... consciousness as self... or self as in consciousness."[26] This sort of identification leads to suffering. But the learned noble disciple does not identify these *khandhas* with self which leads to the cessation of identity and hence suffering. The Buddha also explained the impermanence of the aggregates themselves which also in a way rebuts the existence of any abiding unity (self) existing in the background as the substratum of all these. He say, "this is not mine, this I am not, this is not myself."[27] The aggregates or the *khandhas* i.e. body, feeling, perception, disposition and consciousness are all impermanent. And when one with right knowledge views these as what they really are i.e. impermanent then the mind of that person becomes dispassionate and becomes free from the habit of clinging. Non-clinging leads to steadiness and contentment; and a person is not agitated then. This leads to his *nibbāna* i.e., "destroyed is birth, the holy life has been lived, what has to be done has been done, there is no more for this state of being."[28]

Thus, the Buddha denied that any of the aggregates individually or in combination may be considered to be an ego, self, or soul (*attā*). Whenever one

---

26. SN, 3.22.44.
27. SN, 3.22.44.
28. *Ibid*.

tries to find what is behind this psycho-physical personality or what is binding these aggregates together, one is not able to find anything called self or soul. Rather one only arrives at one or the other component of the aggregate. So, it is erroneous to postulate any real, eternal, abiding unity in the background of the elements that compose up an agent. The Buddha taught that accepting self behind the *khandhas* results in attachment, craving and egoism, which leads to dissatisfaction and hence suffering. This is why he gave the doctrine of *anattā*, i.e. the doctrine that there is no permanent self. With this sort of understanding of one's existence one could be drawn away from egoistic attachments leading to suffering. But nowhere has the Buddha denied the doer of actions, an agent.

At various occasions Buddha is said to not to have answered the questions on the existence of self and remained silent. An encounter between Buddha and Vacchagotta, where the latter asks Buddha whether there is a self that can be cited.[29] Buddha remained silent. Then Vacchagotta asks if that means there is no self. Again Buddha remained silent. Later Buddha explains his silence to his disciple Ānanda as: If he had said there is a self, he would be open to the charge of siding with the eternalists. To say that there is a self does not fit with the Buddha's teaching of impermanence. On the other hand, to say that there is no self is to side with the annihilationist, who rejected any idea of rebirth as untenable. Since the Buddha himself professes a concept of rebirth, the denial of

29. SN, 4.400-401.

the self would only tend to confuse the uneducated. Thus, the Buddha takes the middle view and remains silent.[30]

This middle way the Buddha explained in great detail in dialogue with a *Brahmin*.[31] In response to the question Buddha points at the two extremes that should be avoided: one, the belief that one who performs an action bears the results of that action; the other extreme is the belief in the non-identity of the doer and the experiencer of the fruits of actions. The implication of the Buddha's response is that the person who undergo experiences of the fruits of actions done in one life is neither the same nor different from the person who did the action in the past life. This can mean that the concept of identity that an individual seeks to maintain between the doer and the experiencer is not the correct view according to Buddha. He warns against establishing identity because no one *khandha* as well as the aggregate of the *khandhas* remains the same. They are in a continuous state of flux or becoming.[32] Previous states of affairs only provide conditions for the arising of the subsequent states of affairs, as affirmed by the doctrine of *paṭiccasamuppāda* (dependent co-origination).

Through the network of series of causes, a correlation is established between the deeds and the latter experiencing of their results of actions, between ignorance and desire, on the one hand, and rebirth, on the other. Rebirth therefore

30. SN, 4.44.

31. SN, 2.76.

32. Malalasekera, 'The Individual in Therāvāda Buddhism', p. 146.

conditions rebirth. What is asserted is a locus of points in a changing causal chain, rather than any permanent entity of any kind, which could transmigrate. There is nothing which transmigrates. It is only *kamma* or *saṇkhāra*, a vibrational force, power or energy which goes to the next birth and is the connecting link between the two existences. Till the time there are these tendencies surviving there will be perpetuation of the life.

P.T. Raju raises an objection and says:

> ... it is not clear as to what has been meant by 'body' in Buddhist schools.' Different terms have been used to describe this psycho-physical organism like *puggala*, *nama-rupa*, *pañcaskandha*, including senses, mind, consciousness. In either case, there is much that can be said in favour of this view. Yet, there is a lacuna in the argument. The body may be accepted as the instrument of both cognition and action; but whose instrument is it? It is a guided instrument, not an unguided one; I guide, direct my body and the senses and the organs of action according to my interests. An instrument is utilized and guided by another entity. The 'I' which Buddhism seeks to explain away is missing in the argument; otherwise it presents an important idea.[33]

Thus, Buddha's conception of person needs further explanation. If actions are done by the agent, then is it the case that they are a sort of events which happen due to the presence of certain conditions? Or is it that the guiding agency over and above the aggregate of *khandhas* is required to explain the origin of actions? I think, the former explanation will fit better into the Buddhist framework of the doctrine of impermanence.

---

33. P.T. Raju, *Structural Depths of Indian Thought*, New Delhi: South Asian Publishers, 1985, p. 174.

According to Buddhism, there is no conception of self which transmigrates from one state of existence to another. There is no agent who abandons the *khandhas* from one state of existence to another independently. The advent of the *khandhas* in the next state of existence happens due to the causal relationship of the previous *kammas* to the future *kammas* (*paṭiccasamuppāda*). Therefore, there is no free substantial reality which can be recognised as an agent, but merely a collection of actions.

Thus, we do not find any one substantial entity to whom agency is ascribed in Buddhism. It is only by way of the psychophysical organism that the doing of the action is explained. In the absence of a permanent entity which undergoes all sorts of actions, cognitions, retention, conation etc. the talk of imposing responsibility is equally difficult.

In the next section I will discuss how in the absence of self moral responsibility is understood. For it is very clear from various examples in the *Nikāyas* that everyone had to bear the consequences of one's actions. It is repeatedly said that good actions bring about good results and bad ones results that are bad. Individuals are responsible. But this whole process of fixing reward and punishment is so complex that we should not think that since we cannot know it is not the case. The remainder of this chapter will be devoted to this belief and to the further question of ethical freedom.

III

It is said by the Buddha that one can stop the cycle of birth and death. Now, this raises interesting questions that if the individual is conditioned and determined by their intentions and *kamma* and is capable of terminating these tendencies responsible for suffering and perpetuation of life and attainment of *nibbāna*, then this implies that any individual orperson is not fully determined in the fatalistic sense. So, can we say that there is some sort of freedom that is available to a person to reform his actions and intentions which paves the way for enlightenment?

Buddha explained by way of his discourses and other analogies the complex mechanism of *kamma* where it is difficult and tricky to mould and weave everything in a simplified way to this network of *kamma*. It has been unhesitatingly stressed upon by Buddha that volition is *kamma*. Whether this volition is itself the very source of freedom or not can be analysed. There are several reasons which can be cited for claiming that there is a commitment to some notion of freewill in Buddha's teaching. In discussion of *kamma* (*Devadutta Sutta*), it is said by Buddha that "this evil action was done by you yourself, and you yourself will experience its result."[34] The assumption is that a deed done by a person will bear fruits only to that person. Evil brings evil, good brings good. Moreover, throughout his ethical discourses Buddha urged and motivated people

34. MN, 3.180-3.183.

on a regular basis to do things in a certain way and to refrain from doing this is certain other ways. Even at the time of his death, he said he felt he could not leave without addressing his people/disciples and said: "Therefore, *Ānanda*, you should live as islands unto yourselves, being your own refuge, with no one else as your refuge, with the *Dhamma* as an island, with the *Dhamma* as your refuge, with no other refuge."[35] In *Dhammapada* it is said "by effort and heedfulness, discipline and self-mastery, let the wise one make for himself an island which no flood can overwhelm."[36] Further it is said, "by oneself is evil done; by oneself is one defiled. By oneself is evil left undone; by oneself is one made pure. Purity and impurity depend on oneself; no one can purify another. One, indeed, is patron of oneself; oneself is one's own guide. Therefore, restrain yourself, as a merchant, a noble steed."[37] Buddha repeatedly gives the refrains that it is entirely in one's hands to reform actions and the intentions behind them. Though one carries the baggage of past impressions which in a way conditions one's desires, volitions, choices and actions, still Buddha says that a person with wisdom gained from the understanding of the impermanence of everything including *khandhas* has the potential and power to change or overcome one's unwanted intentions and desires. This clearly shows that, Buddha did not define the existence of a human personality by rendering it as a puppet in the hands of fate. Nor was the Buddha ready to absolutely remove control on the choices one makes. That is absolute

---

35. DN, 2.100-102., *Mahaparinibbāna Sutta*.
36. DHP2.25, p. 26.
37. *Ibid.*, 12.165, p. 48.

freedom to act was not acceptable to Buddha. He taught that instead of going to any extreme of either absolute determinism or absolute freedom, one should follow the middle path where a person is both free and determined. Free in the sense of improving the future states of existence and determined in the sense of being conditioned by the play of the previous life impressions producing tendencies. Another reason that pushes for Buddha's acceptance of some form of freewill is that Buddhist texts are full of examples where people are held morally responsible for their behaviour and deeds and responsibility presupposes freewill.

Also, Buddha vehemently rejected the fatalism of the Ājīvikas. Makkhāli Gosālā, the leader of Ājīvika believed in the principle of absolute determinism. He said:

> ...there is no cause or condition for the purification of beings, they are purified without cause or condition. There is no self power or other power, there is no power in humans, no strength or force, no vigour or exertion. All beings, all living things, all creatures, all that lives is without control, without power and strength, they experience the fixed course of pleasure and pain through six kinds of rebirth... therefore there is no such thing as: by this discipline or practice or austerity or holy life will bring unripened kamma to fruition, or will gradually make this ripened kamma go away. Neither of these things is possible, because pleasure and pain have been measured out with a measure limited by the round of birth and death, and there is neither increase nor decrease, neither excellence nor inferiority. Just as a ball of string when thrown runs till it is all unravelled, so fools and wise run on and circle on till they make an end of suffering.[38]

To this Buddha replied:

> there is power, energy, manly strength, manly endurance. It is not the case that all beings, all living things, all creatures, all souls are

38. DN, 1.55, *Sāmaññaphala Sutta*.

> without mastery, power and energy, or that moulded by destiny, circumstance, and nature, they experience pleasure and pain in the six classes.[39]

Buddha rejected fatalism because if anyone were so determined or hard wired that they had no scope to choose and change their nature of actions, then no one would pursue the path of liberation. The Buddha did not accept this and gave full power and mastery in the hands of the individual to achieve the success of liberation. Thus, it seems clear from the above cited reasons that for the Buddha worldly existence cannot be without action and bearing the responsibility for its outcome. Can a compatibilist position be ascribed to Buddha's understanding of one's being heir to one's *kamma,* i.e., a person oneself being responsible for one's state of existence? A compatibilist view of freewill holds, as explained previously in the introduction, that an individual is both free and determined. Free in the sense that the choices one makes are determined by the agent themself from within without their determination from outside. That is a person is not coerced or constrained by external factors. However, one may have no control over one's physical and psychological makeup which is transmitted to one by causes external to one.[40] Several elements of Buddhist thought might be interpreted as implying a commitment to determinism like the doctrine of *kamma* and the theory of dependent origination. As when the Buddha says:

---

39. *Ibid.*, 1.61, *Sāmaññaphala Sutta.*

40. See entry on 'Freewill' in *Concise Routledge Encyclopedia of Philosophy,* London: Routledge, 2000, pp. 293-294.

> If, sometime or other, at the end of a long period, that fool comes back to the human state, it is into a low family that he is reborn - into a family of outcasts or hunters or bamboo-workers or cartwrights or scavengers ... he misconducts himself in body, speech, and mind, and having done that, on the dissolution of the body, after death, he reappears in a state of deprivation, in an unhappy destination, in perdition, even in hell. Bhikkhus, suppose a gambler at the very first unlucky throw loses his child and his wife and all his property and furthermore goes into bondage himself, yet an unlucky throw such as that is negligible; it is a far more unlucky throw when a fool who misconducts himself in body, speech, and mind, on the dissolution of the body, after death, reappears in a state of deprivation, in an unhappy destination, in perdition, even in hell. This is the complete perfection of the fool's grade.[41]

This might be thought to imply that our actions at a given point of time are determined by our past actions. However, Buddha rejected such a strong form of determinism that all our actions are due to past deeds.[42] In Buddhism, *kamma* is very much a causal concept i.e. our actions in the present causally affect our well-being in the future. But as it has been stated earlier, the specific ways in which *kamma* works are complex and difficult to understand, and the doctrine does not seem to be that our actions in the present strictly determine our actions in the future. Thus, *kamma* as such would not seem to be the plausible basis for attributing to Buddhism that all our actions are causally determined by prior events.

The other most common reason for interpreting Buddhist thought as committed to a form of causal determinism is the doctrine of dependent origination: "when

---

41. MN, 3.169-170, p. 1021.

42. AN, 1.174.

this exists, that comes to be; with the arising of this, that arises. When this does not exist, that does not come to be; with the cessation of this, that ceases."[43] However, this sort of interpretation is challenged by many thinkers. There are various variations of this doctrine in the *Pāli* canon and the *Abhidhamma* schools. Several grounds for non determinist position have been proposed. One is that it is not a theory of determinism but of conditioning. This dependent origination theory though is the doctrine of universal causation, may be interpreted in probabilistic rather than deterministic terms. Buddha always taught that one can bring about cessation to one's sufferings. Determinist interpretations may imply an unwarranted imposition of mechanical causation on the doctrine of dependent arising presupposing strict determinism into a context in which causality was more likely to have been understood in terms of an organic model of causality that need not involve determinism.[44] Lastly, the dependent arising was given in Buddha's scheme of liberation as a basic practical presupposition and not as a metaphysical theory. One can change one's conditions which are responsible for one's sufferings by overcoming conditions responsible for it. From this perspective we can say that the theory of dependent origination was a forward looking measure for mastery, empowerment,

---

43. MN, 2.32., The longer version is given in section I paragraph 3.

44. Karin I. Meyers, 'Free Persons Empty Selves: Freedom and Agency in the Light of the Two Truths', in *Freewill, Agency and Selfhood in Indian Philosophy*, (eds.) Matthew R. Dasti and Edwin F. Bryant, Oxford: Oxford University Press, 2014, pp. 41-67.

improving our lives by being virtuous and not a backward looking argument to impose hard determinism in the world view.

In modern times, philosophers have shown sympathy with the compromise between fatalism and absolute free will. Dennett, independently though in parallel to the Buddhist idea of compatibilism, developed an argument in order to set a polemic against the fatalistic and deterministic viewpoints. Dennett shows the difference between the terms 'determined; and 'inevitability'. Likewise if determinism is true then all that human face is an 'inevitable' outcome is not same as to say that if determinism is true then all that human face is 'determined'. The difference arises because the notion of inevitability is packed with this absolute powerlessness of the agent to change the course of events making the performer redundant. However, to be determined still allows the will to change the course of the action under certain causal factors.[45] We infer from Dennett's position that even though the Buddha maintained the role of past *karma* as the deciding feature in human actions, nonetheless, humans can act wilfully out of those actions.

Now, since the stage has been set that how determinism and freedom can be said to be acceptable in Buddhist thought we gather confidence to explore some of the compatibilist positions. It is felt by many scholars that a compatibilist model of freedom fits into the Buddha's scheme of freedom to act. Luis O Gomez utilizes the discussion on dependent origination to make way for

---

45. Daniel Dennett, *Freedom Evolves,* New York: Penguin Books, 2003, p. 57.

freedom of the will avoiding the two extremes of annihilationists and the eternalists. Both the views are fatal for the doctrine of liberation for either there will be no respite from the effects of actions done or the effects of actions will be chance happenings. For Gomez, if causation is only accepted as "continuity without fatalism"[46] then there is no problem with accepting freedom to action. But if this causation is accepted as the only explanation for human condition, then it will take us to the extreme end of eternalism where there is no relief from regularity. What could be the way out of this problem where reconciliation can happen between indeterminism and determinism? The Buddhist answer would be of course the middle path between these two extremes. Gomez suggests that "if by causation is meant weak conditioning, then perhaps it does solve it, but if total conditioning of the series is intended, then the Buddhist would be no better than the *ājīvikas*."[47] He uses the phrase 'continuity without fatalism' in order to show the middle way adopted by the Buddha between absolute freedom and fatalism. Such a position for attainment of *Nirvāṇa* for Gomez would be a weak form of *kriyāvāda*, which comes in contrast to strong form of *kriyāvāda* which is tantamount to absolute freedom on one hand and with *akriyavāda* (non-action) on the other.[48] This point is taken up by Peter Harvey to highlight the conditional aspect of an agent.

46. Luis O Gomez, 'Freewill Question in the Nikāyas', *Philosophy East and West,* Vol.25 (1), 1975, p. 87.

47. *Ibid.*, p. 88.

48. *Ibid.*, p. 82.

Peter Harvey[49] understands that according to Buddhism freedom of the will on the part of the agent constitutes in the capacity of an agent to reflect and assess the moral suitability of any action before its performance. One may be conditioned but not absolutely determined. So, one can regulate, modify, change one's willings and choice of actions with the broader understanding of the impermanent nature of the things in existence. There is scope for new development as not only an agent but also his interaction with the environment is changing or evolving. This opens a space where with the understanding of the factors which condition oneself, there is the possibility to revise one's scheme of conditioned existence. Thus, the more there is desire, greed and delusion, the lesser freedom to act there will be. Awareness about one's conditioning factors enhances the scope of freedom to act, "replacing limiting unskilful conditioning by more open-ended skilful conditioning."[50] And the eight fold path given by the Buddha is the refuge to enhance one's freedom by overcoming one's passions and desires. Thus, responsibility for the actions done can be attributed to the agents for the actions done by them are intentional. And there will be no contradiction which challenges the existence of both freedom as well as determinism.

Asaf Federman also somewhat resounds Peter Harvey's understanding of freedom of the will in Buddhism. For him, with the doctrine of *kamma* and

49. Peter Harvey, 'Freedom of the Will in the Light of Therāvāda Buddhism', *Journal of Buddhist Ethics*, Vol.14, 2007, p. 84.

50. *Ibid.*, p. 85.

anattā (absence of soul), only a compatibilist model of freedom makes sense. On the one hand, existence of freewill outside the causal nexus created by an individual is denied and on the other hand, at the same time it is asserted that choices are determined by the agent's desire and intention, which have to take responsibility for the same. Further, the choice of right action doesn't have its origin in some supernatural power or god. It is very much an outcome of wisdom and contemplation over the possible outcomes of any action. Thus, wisdom clarified by the knowledge of four Noble Truths enables the exercise of freewill. This freedom can be enhanced and developed. "What limits freewill is not causality itself but various mental compulsions."[51] It is the acquired ability for reflection and contemplation which leads to the making of wise choices that defines freewill according to Buddha. This very enhancement of freedom is in conformity with the path of enlightenment of freedom. Federman is not alone in converging the free action and the path involved to achieve freedom together. Agency along with its dependent momentary existence is endorsed by various interpretors of the Buddha.

One such position has been developed by Mark Siderits called "paleo-compatibilism" [52] where he utilizes the distinction between ultimate and conventional truth to present his case. In his view, at the ultimate level, there is

---

51. Asaf Federman, 'What Kind of Freewill Did the Buddha Teach', *Philosophy East and West,* Vol. 60 (1), 2010, p. 15.

52. Mark Siderits, 'Paleo-compatibilism and Buddhist Reductionism', *Sophia,* Vol. 47 (1), 2008, pp. 29-42.

no self or persons; there are only causally related series of interdependent physical and mental events. At this level psychological determinism is true: each of these events is causally determined by prior events. At the level of conventional truth, instead of complex series of interdependent events, we speak of selves or persons as distinct entities with identity through time we employ the concept of agent for practical purpose to control human behaviour by assuming that agents freely choose their actions and so may be held responsible for performing them through rewards and punishments. Thus, at the conventional level there is an understanding of a person- as deliberating, choosing, willing, acting, evaluating- processes which he does freely without determination from prior causes outside of him. At the ultimate level of truth, there are no persons and so it is neither true nor false that persons act freely and are responsible for their actions. Siderits maintains that this sort of compatibilist position is acceptable in early Buddhism which allows for determinism as well as freedom and responsibility. But Siderits' position has been objected to as it is a common phenomena that people appear to be more determined by their emotions and attachments at the conventional level and at this level freedom is only apparent and not real. Then how do we make sense of responsibility.

Karin Meyers has developed an alternative compatibilist model to answer these objections. She says that:

> ...goal-oriented action, effort and initiative involved in taking up and practicing the path seems to require, psychologically speaking,

> a certain kind of self-grasping, specifically, the kind of self-grasping in which one regards oneself as an autonomous agent. From an impersonal perspective, we might say that this is just a glitch in the information-processing mechanism such that there is a mismatch between how things really are and how the mechanism responds. But it also seems to be the case that this process cannot be reversed without the energy produced by this delusion of autonomy. In personal terms, this is the energy or empowerment we feel when we take responsibility for our situation and commit to doing something about it.[53]

Meyers quotes that when a Brahmin approaches the Buddha and claims that nothing is done by oneself (*attakāra*) or others (*parakāra*), the Buddha asks "how one who has himself stepped forward can say this, for isn't there an element (*dhātu*) of initiative (*arabbha*), exertion (*nikkama*), striving (*parākkama)*, resistance (*thama*), stability (*thiṭi*), and undertaking (*upakkama*), when one steps forward or retreats?"[54] This might not imply an absolutely free choice, but it does suggest the psychological importance of maintaining a view of oneself as an autonomous agent responsible for one's deeds. Delusion of freedom can take us so far that one can gain control over one's body, speech and mind. It won't do, however, to simply let go from the outset and whole heartedly embrace the impersonal view of action and abandon responsibility. So, a person grows his freedom as the strength of self-grasping loosens by taking responsibility for one's actions. Gradually then no conscious effort is required once self grasping looses enough that action becomes spontaneous not being guided by any negative factors. Thus for Meyers from ultimate

53. Meyers, 'Free Persons Empty Selves', p. 61.

54. *Ibid.,* AN, 3.337-338.

perspective there is no freewill, because there are no persons but only a continuous flow of *dhammas*. But conventional freedom is significant to push a person to the ultimate freedom, i.e., liberation.

Another compatibilist model has been proposed by B.A.Wallace where he says that Buddha avoided the two extremes of nihilism and eternalism, and followed the middle path. Similarly in these matters of freedom and determinism he neither advocates absolute determinism nor indeterminism but the mid way which is beyond determinism and indeterminism. He says:

> There is freedom in the present moment to view the world in accordance with different conceptual frameworks, and this is where free will may enter into our experience. By shifting our way of framing appearances and making sense of them within our cognitive framework, we alter the very nature of the world as it arises from moment to moment relative to our way of viewing it. For example, a natural calamity may be viewed either as an unmitigated adversity, or it may be seen as an opportunity to cultivate deeper compassion. The categories of 'adversity' and 'felicity' are ones we superimpose on experience; they are not absolutely thrust on us from outside.[55]

Wallace believes that in Buddhism by conceptually designating events in ways that support virtue rather than habitual mental afflictions, one alters the world one inhabits; and this constitutes a fundamental freedom of choice. As long as one is acting from the dimension of ordinary, dualistic consciousness, the most one can hope for is to condition the mind in ways that are conducive to one's own and others' genuine happiness. Only with the breakthrough to pristine

55. B.A. Wallace, 'A Buddhist View of Freewill', *Journal of Consciousness Studies*, 18, No. 3-4, 2011, pp. 217-33.

awareness does one discover a dimension of freedom that is beyond the intellect and beyond the realm of causal conditioning. Wallace's view can be seen as supporting compatibilist position where he acknowledges that a person has the freedom to perceive and choose among different conceptual frameworks. It is in our control to choose what attitude one wants to keep for any life situation.

Putting together the views of the above mentioned scholars it can be said that Dennett, though he does not make any comment about Buddhism, accepts freedom at the level of determination of will to choose and change one's course of action. Gomez describes his position by discussing the doctrine of dependent origination and by making a way for freedom of the will through it, thereby avoiding the two extremes of annihilationism and eternalism. Harvey also utilized the theory of dependent arising to talk about freedom, where consciousness of one's conditioning factors enhances one's freedom to act. Federman echoes Harvey's view and takes it further by remarking that causality does not limit freedom, but various mental compulsions do. Siderits accepts compatibilism by showing that the person at the conventional level is taken to be capable of choosing, willing and acting freely for ascribing responsibility at the practical level. Meyers talks of the idea of self-grasping where one regards oneself as an autonomous psychological agent, responsible for one's deeds, despite being under various mechanisms. Lastly, Wallace finds freedom at the level of thought to choose and alter among the available conceptual setups. Awareness of the ill effects of forming judgements enhances one's freedom to act. Thus, it can broadly be seen that compatibilist model is the best interpretation of freedom which defines the scope of responsibility in the background of determinism in early Buddhist philosophy and all the above mentioned scholars have accepted it. In agreement with their views and keeping in mind the Buddhist notion of *kamma* and dependent origination as I had explained and analysed earlier, I feel that the compatibilist understanding of freedom is the most appropriate explanation for the Buddhist understanding of freedom of the agent. Consequently, an individual has the 'freedom to' cultivate *Sīla*, *Samādhi,* and *Paññā* for removing the root cause *tanhā* which perpetuates the wheel of life and death (suffering). The agent then with their own will or volition bring the cessation of the 'will to be born' eventually leading to 'freedom from' suffering.

Summing up the chapter, we may conclude that the Buddha accepted intention and anything born out of it as *kamma*. Intention or volition is ascribed to a person *(puggala)* who is an aggregate of conditions (*khandhas*). There is no self as a permanent entity who is the doer/agent that transmigrates to the next birth. It is only the *saṇkhāra* or dispositions of *kamma* of the past life that make up the causes and conditions for the arising of the individual person. This individual exercises agency at the empirical level till the time he/she is ignorant i.e. has not realised of the Noble Truths. From the transcendental point of view the agent is nothing over and above the collection of certain conditions. These conditions when co-located give rise to agency without any abiding entity controlling and regulating the operations of mind, body and speech. This sort of agent (comprising of five factors) in early Buddhist thought can be said to be both determined and free to choose actions. Indoctrinating the middle path, early Buddhism creates the possibility of following the ethical path and reforming one's deeds and intentions without going to the extremes of absolute determination on the one hand and absolute freedom on the other. When one's intentions are purified, one's actions become detached. This detachment leads to the realisation that the identity of the individual as an essential self is mistaken. And this leads to freedom from bondage. Thus, it is interesting to note that the conception of agent at the empirical level is necessary to understand that ultimately there is no eternal being that undergoes pleasurable or painful experiences. When this ignorance is dispelled with the understanding of dependent arising, there is nothing left to be known. One is then free from all conditions.

IV

Karma, Agency and Freedom in Sāṃkhya-Yoga

The Sāṃkhya school is accepted as one of the oldest systems of Indian philosophical thought dating back to *Upaniṣadic* times. Sage Kapila is credited as being the founder of this school as well as the author of *Sāṃkhya Sūtras*. The peculiarity of this school lies in maintaining two distinct fundamental mutually exclusive realities, namely, *prakṛti* and *puruṣa*. *Prakṛti* is one, ever mutable: it evolves the material world out of itself. The dynamics of *prakṛti* are governed by the interactions of the three *guṇas* viz., *sattva*, *rajas* and *tamas*. *Puruṣa* is pure consciousness, many, immutable, without form, without attachment and inactive. The apparent conjunction between individual *puruṣa* and *prakṛti* brings about the existence of *jīva*. Though Sāṃkhya and Yoga eventually emanated as two of the six systems of Indian philosophy, they were not considered distinct in the earlier period.[1] The ancient available doxographies do not identify Yoga as a separate school. The Yoga philosophy is said to have accentuated Sāṃkhya philosophy with praxis, a pre-requisite for reflective discrimination between two absolute realities, viz. *prakṛti* and *puruṣa*, a discrimination crucial for liberation.

1 . Radhakrishnan writes "In the *Mahabharata*, the Sāṃkhya and the Yoga are used as complimentary aspects of one whole, signifying theory and practice, philosophy and religion". S. Radhakrishnan, *Indian Philosophy*, Vol. 2, Oxford University Press, 2010,p.312.

P.T. Raju writes "the Sāṃkhya and the Yoga were combined and formed the Sāṃkhya-Yoga school to which metaphysics and epistemology were mostly supplied by the Sāṃkhya and the practice of meditation for the final discrimination of the self from the non-self was explained by the yoga". P.T. Raju, *Structural Depths of Indian Thought*, New Delhi: South Asian Publishers, 1985, p. 305.

In this chapter I shall be discussing on agency, *karma* and freedom in the Sāṃkhya-Yoga tradition. Some selective sources have been consulted and referred to. These are namely, the *Sāṃkhyakārika* (SK) of Iśvarakṛṣṇa with three of its commentaries by Gauḍapāda (SK,G), *Yuktidīpikā* (SK,Y) and *Sāṃkhya-Tattva-Kaumudi* of Vācaspatimiśra (STK); the *Yoga Sūtras* (YS) of Patañjali with some of its principal commentaries by Vyāsa and Vācaspatimiśra; the *Sāṃkhya Sūtras* (SSū) of Kapila and its commentary by Aniruddha (SSū,A). In order to discuss the theory of *karma*, agency and freedom of action in this chapter, I shall be hence looking at the literature of both Sāṃkhya and Yoga schools.

This chapter accordingly discusses the nature of the agent, the agency aspect from the Sāṃkhya-Yoga perspective and the questions that can be raised in the background of the determination of one's life and its experiences by *karma* of past and present to address issues of freedom.

I

The theory of *karma* can be well inferred from the first aphorism of *Sāṃkhyakārikā*. It states that suffering is a pervasive and natural predicament. Sāṃkhya and Yoga accept the very embodiment of *puruṣa* to be suffering.

Interestingly, in Sāṃkhya both enjoyment and misery are considered to be nothing but suffering which each individual self must realise and transcend. The realisation of suffering drives the individual self to attain freedom from it. In order to understand the nature of suffering the Sāṃkhya philosophy explicates its threefold classification (*dukhtraya*). They are: the intrinsic (*ādhyātmika*) constituting of bodily disorders and mental suffering resulting from emotional and passionate activity, the extrinsic (*ādhibhautika*) suffering is determined by beings, beasts, birds, reptiles and inanimate things and the supernatural (*ādhidaivika*) suffering inflicted by planets, ghosts, demons and the natural elements.[2] The ultimate goal of human life is to overcome these sufferings. The existence of suffering leads to action (*karma*). This can be explained by the fact that suffering incessantly leads to desire for the cessation of suffering. This in turn leads one to undertake action to achieve good (*puruṣārtha*) for oneself. For e.g. when someone is hungry, satisfaction of hunger by taking food is good for the person. But the means adopted for the satiation of hunger will result into accruing merit and demerit. This flow of action can be understood in the following words of Vācaspatimiśra quoted by K.R. Rao : "Every one who deals with an object first intuits it, then reflects upon it, then appropriates it, then resolves "this is to be done by me", and then proceeds to act".[3] Since, the Sāṃkhya system believes in multiplicity of *puruṣas* (*puruṣabahutva*), therefore, each individual's merit and demerit subsequently differs on account of their respective actions.[4]

---

2. STK, pp. 2-4.
3. K.Ramakrishna Rao, 'Perception, Cognition and Consciousness in Classical Hindu Psychology', *Journal of Consciousness Studies*, Vol.12, No.3, 2005, p. 13.
4. G.J. Larson, 'Krishna Chandra Bhattacharya and the Plurality of *Puruṣas* (*Puruṣabahutva*) in Sāṃkya', *Journal of Indian Council of Philosophical Research*, Vol. 10(1), 1992, p. 96.

In order to understand the nature of the embodiment of the individual self, it is a prerequisite to know the nature of *prakṛti* and its process of evolution. At the primordial level there is a perfect equilibrium of the three qualities (*guṇas*). They are: *sattva* which is light and illuminating, *rajas* is energy and cause of activity and motion; and *tamas* is heavy and obstructing.[5] The evolution of *prakṛti* begins with the disturbance of this equilibrium. The homogeneity of the three qualities of *prakṛti* together become heterogenous due to their inherent potential to overpower each other (*virūpapariṇāma*). The first evolute of *prakṛti* is *mahat* (the great). It is the highest and subtlest form of matter. Mahat has two aspects: the cosmic and the psychological counterpart in the individual called intellect (*buddhi*). *Buddhi* is subtler than *manas*. From *mahat* arises *ahaṃkāra*, which is the individual 'I', ego principle. *Ahaṃkāra* is a supra-physical principle of individuation, thoroughly informed by spiritual effulgence and transformed beyond recognition.[6] Then emerges mind (*manas*) and five sense organs (eyes, ears, nose, tongue and skin), five motor organs (hands, feet, mouth, anus and the sex organ), and five subtle elements (generic essence of the function of sense organs). Here mind is a central organ which facilitates the functioning of the organs of knowledge (sense organs) and action (motor organs) of the individual soul.[7] Further, the embodiment of the individual *puruṣa* is due to the evolution of *prakṛti*. *Prakṛti* in the form of subtle

5. S.N. Dasgupta, *A History of Indian Philosophy*, Vol.1, Delhi: Motilal Banarsidass, 2010, p. 224.

6. SSū, *Pradhāna-Kāryadhaya* 2.19-20, pp. 201-2.(Nyāya view criticised)

7. Chatterjee &Datta, *An Introduction to Indian Philosophy*, Calcutta: Calcutta University Press, 2012, p. 269.

body (*liṅgaśarīra*) is eternal comprising of mind (*manas*), intellect (*buddhi*) and ego (*ahaṃkāra*), ten sense organs and five subtle essences, devoid of experiences transmigrates endowed with dispositions (*bhāvas*).[8] These dispositions are of two kinds: natural or innate and incidental or adventitious. At the beginning of the evolution, subtle body is equipped with innate tendencies of virtue, wisdom, dispassion and power. On the other hand, incidental dispositions are the result of the efforts made by the individual selves like virtue and vice, wisdom and ignorance, dispassion and passion; and power and weakness.[9] On the one hand, by practising virtue there is spiritual upgradation in the scale of beings towards liberation, on the other hand vices lead to degradation or downward movement to lower realms. The wisdom or discriminative knowledge leads to release (*apavarga*). Ignorance on the other hand leads to passionate activity or bondage.[10]

However, this subtle body when endowed with unseen potency[11] takes the form of gross body. The gross body unlike the subtle body (*liṅgaśarīra*) is sheer materiality. The subtle body is neither born nor dies whereas the gross body does. The subtle body is the cause/source of the gross body.[12] It is the subtle body that transmigrates not the gross body. The individual self (*jīva*) enjoys/

---

8. STK, pp. 122-23.
9. STK, Vācaspati Miśra on *kārikā* LVIII, p. 128.
10. *Ibid.*, pp. 129-130.
11. Unseen potency will be discussed later in the chapter.
12. Sāṃkhya is sympathetic to the *satkāryavāda* theory of causation where the effect is accepted to be contained in the cause. Likewise, the gross body subsists in the subtle body.

suffers through the gross body at the phenomenal level.[13] The actions done by the *jīva* produces merit and demerit leading to the creation of dispositions (*bhāvas*). When the actions done are the result of the gross body then these results should also belong to the gross body. But it is said that dispositions attach with the subtle body and travel with it to the next birth. Now the question arises how can the dispositions (*bhāvas*) be connected with the subtle body? It is said that since the subtle body is the foundation of the gross body, it becomes invested with the dispositions pertaing to the gross body. We can understand this analogically with the example of cloth and Campaka flower. Just as the cloth when in contact with Campaka flowers absorbs its fragrance, in the same way the subtle body gets invested with the dispositions when in contact with the gross body. Even when the gross body perishes the dispositions do not and therefore transmigrate with the subtle body. This is evident that even when the cloth gets separated from the flowers it continues to bear fragrance.[14] In this way it can be understood that this association leads to continuous cycles of birth and death till the time the baggage of merit and demerit known as *adṛṣṭa* in Sāṃkhya is exhausted with the realisation of discriminative knowledge i.e. *puruṣa* is distinct from *prakrti*.[15]

---

13. Jadunath Sinha, *Indian Philosophy*, Vol. 2, Delhi: Motilal Banarsidass, 1999, p. 22.
14. STK, Vācaspatimiśra on *kārikā* XL, p. 124.
15. SK, LV, *Classical Sāṃkhya,* (tr.) G.J. Larson, Delhi: Motilal Banarsidas, 1969, p. 277.

The above discussion on the emobodiment of *puruṣa* unravels that it is in strict accordance with past life impressions *(saṃskāras)* and tendencies *(vāsanās)* that are preactive and determine the cycle of birth and death of an individual. This embodiment of *puruṣa* is described as the *bogāyatana*[16] i.e. a frame in which certain pre-determined affective experiences, whether pleasurable or painful are to be felt. The senses of cognition and of action owe their peculiarity in each organism to the unseen power *(adṛṣṭa)* which is a super-physical prenatal force. The philosophers of the Sāṃkhya school refuse to look upon the *adṛṣṭa* as a force inherent in the self. This does not mean that *adṛṣṭa* as the evolutionary factor, is to be identified with gross matter or anything grossly material, rather its identification lies with the subtle body. Thus according to this school *karma* is understood both as actions and unseen potency produced by the results from the performance of the actions. With the acquisition of discriminating knowledge, the origination of merit and demerit can be stopped, which further results in gradual exhaustion of *adṛṣṭa*.

II

The observations of the locus of unseen potency (*adṛṣṭa*) in Sāṃkhya makes clear the process of individuation. This individuation is responsible for the multiplicity of agents in Sāṃkhya thought. The system of thought is built on the foundation of two discrete and ultimately independent, irreducible ontological

---

16. Sinha, *Indian Philosophy,* Vol. 1, p. 43.

entities, *prakṛti* and *puruṣa*. *Puruṣa* is pure, conscious, eternal, and immutable. *Prakṛti* is the unconscious matter underpinning the physical world of change. There are no psychic functions inherent in the *puruṣa*. It is over and above the entire manifest and unmanifest world characterised as being, "... a witness (*sākṣitvam*), possessed of isolation or freedom (*kaivalyam*), indifferent (*mādhyasthyam*), a spectator who sees (*draṣṭṛtvam*) and inactive (*akartṛbhāva*)".[17] The self is concealed by intellect (*buddhi*), ego (*ahaṃkāra*) and mind (*manas*) which are the evolutes of *prakṛti* and are distinct, separable and inanimate coverings of *Puruṣa*. When it is untwined from its coverings, the released *ātman/puruṣa* itself, in its pure autonomous state (*kaivalya*), is dispossessed of intentionality. *Prakṛti* is unconscious but dynamic and *puruṣa* is conscious but inactive. This raises an interesting question that in this dualistic type of metaphysics foundational to Sāṃkhya-Yoga, who is the agent of action?

The common understanding of an agent as I have mentioned in previous chapters, is one who has the ability to perform actions by undergoing change and modification. Agency presupposes the potential to make choices. An agent is one thus who undergoes certain sort of modifications to bring about a change in the outer scheme of the world or be responsive to the inner or outer stimuli. Also the agent includes "some form of discriminative and determinative

17. SK, XIX, p.183.

faculties to adequately select the desirable choices between options."[18] All such potential change cannot be brought about by *puruṣa* when it is said to be eternal and immutable i.e. something which does not undergo change. Then in such a situation *puruṣa* cannot be said to be the agent (*kartā*). *Puruṣa* is distinct from anything material (composed of *guṇas*). So, one is left with only the inanimate material principle *prakṛti* to look for agency. Sāṃkhya philosophers have found agent in *prakṛti* alone. It is accepted as unconscious but inherently dynamic. Being an unconscious principle how can *prakṛti* be an agent? The very acceptance of this fact has been a constant source of objection and criticism from other systems like Nyāya and Advaita Vedānta.[19] But Sāṃkhya thinkers have built up arguments with analogies to refute any objections raised. They have explained activity in *prakṛti* by relating consciousness with matter. But this relation is only a facade and not an actual transformation. It is their proximity that is responsible and is clarified. In *Sāṃkhyakārikā* XX it is said that "Therefore, the non-intelligent *liṅga* becomes as if intelligent on account of its contact with that (Spirit) and although the activity belongs to the attributes yet the indifferent (Spirit) seems as if it were an agent"[20]. Thus the *kārika* clarifies that the *puruṣa* is not the agent. Gauḍapāda, the commentator on *Sāṃkhyakārikā* presents an objection to this in the following way: "if the spirit (*puruṣa*) is non-

18. Edwin F. Bryant, 'Agency in Sāṃkhya and Yoga', *Freewill, agency and Selfhood in Indian Philosophy,* (ed.) Dasti and Bryant, New York: Oxford University Press, 2014, p. 20.

19. See chapter on '*Karma*, Agency and Freedom in AdvaitaVedānta'.

20. SK,G, Gauḍapāda on *kārikā* XX, p.31.

agent, then how does it exercise volition — 'I will practice virtue. I will not practice vice'. Therefore, it is an agent."[21] To this he replies by giving an analogy; just like an innocent man who gets arrested along with a gang of thieves, is considered one of them, in the same way Spirit or *puruṣa* under the proximity of dynamic Nature or *prakṛti* is taken to be an agent, despite not being one. Further, he also cites another analogy of a jar and water. Just like the surface of jar becomes hot when filled with hot water and cold when filled with cold water, though in reality it is neither; in the same way, *puruṣa* appears as though it is the agent with the proximity of *prakṛti* but it is not so.

Further, Gauḍapāda, in order to explain this perplexed relationship between *puruṣa* and *prakṛti*, illustrates it by presenting another analogy of a lame man and blind man respectively. He says:

> That union of both should be considered to be like that of a lame man with a blind man. For e.g., one man is lame, the other is blind. These two men were travelling with difficulty; the caravan was attacked by the robbers in the forest; these two were deserted by their friends and wandered haphazardly; in course of their wandering they encountered each other. This reunion of theirs, on account of each relying on the words of the other, serves the purpose of walking and seeing. The blind man mounted the lame man on his shoulders. Thus the blind man walks by the road shown by the layman mounted on the former's body, and the layman (walks) mounted on the blind man's body. Similarly, the spirit like the layman has the power of contemplation, but not of action. The nature like the blind man has the power of action, but not of contemplation. And just as there will be separation of the blind man from the lame man, after their mutual object of reaching the desired for-spot is achieved, so the Nature also ceases to act

21. *Ibid.*

> after bringing about the release of the Spirit; and the Spirit becomes isolated after comtemplating the Nature. After their mutual object is gained, separation will come about.[22]

This is the way the association of the *puruṣa* and *prakṛti* is to be understood. Objections are raised by opponents for the conception of '*puruṣa* as the agent'. In response so as to reject the ascription of agency to the *puruṣa*, *Yuktidīpikā* commentary on *Sāṃkhyakārikā* gives an explanation:

> *Puruṣa* or consciousness is a seer because of being conscious. It is inactive because of its being non-productive. Therefore, it is devoid of activities. Moreover, consciousness is inactive due to its being conscious and of unmixed form, for activity is found in nonconscious objects and objects of mixed nature. It cannot be maintained that consciousness may be active because it is all pervasive like primordial materiality, because the activity of primordial materiality is due to unconsciousness, which is not found in consciousness. Nor should it be argued here that consciousness created bodies merely through thinking, because the possibility of thinking or resolution is already refuted in the case of consciousness.[23]

Agents are capable of producing actions, which in turn makes the individual self undergo some internal change or to bring some change in the external affair of things. This leads to its amalgamation with other entities and thereby undergoes change. If activity is inherent in the self then its eternal nature gets compromised. All this implies that action can only occur in the world of mixture and change, not in any changeless entity like *puruṣa*. With no internal parts and

22. *Ibid.*,p.33

23. Karl H. Potter, *Encyclopedia of Indian Philosophy: Sāṃkhya*, Vol. 4, Delhi: Motilal Banarsidass, 1987, p. 259.

nothing mixed in with it, *puruṣa* produces nothing from itself, and likewise can never change.

Agency in the Sāṃkhya perspective has to be consigned to an entity other than *puruṣa* and Sāṃkhya assigns this function either to *buddhī*, its covering of discrimination, or to the second evolute emanating from *prakṛti*, ego *(ahaṃkāra)*. [24] *Buddhi*, *ahaṃkāra* and *manas* cover the *puruṣa* like a multilayered lampshade covers a bulb: "the ego is the agent, not the *puruṣa*".[25] Aniruddha clarifies that "Here, the intelligence (really) belongs to the Spirit; therefore, the *liṇga* viz. *Mahat* and the rest, coming into contact with the reflection of the intelligent (Spirit), becomes as if intelligent."[26]

For Sāṃkhya, cognition happens when *buddhi* conjoins with the ego, the first evolute of *prakṛti* encasing the *puruṣa*. *Buddhi* has the capacity/potency and is instrumental in determination/discernment of the choices made by the agent. Therefore, Sāṃkhya ascribes agency to *buddhi*.

Will or intellect *(buddhi)* is also the abode of knowledge (*jñāna*) and the behaviour regulating functions like virtue, detachment and possession of power to choose and enact simultaneously. Nyāya has challenged the Sāṃkhya position of the agency. Nyāya ascribes agency and other psychological qualities to the

---

24. SK, XXIV, p.267
25. SS, A, vi.54, p. 296.
26. *Ibid.*

self, while simultaneously preserving its changelessness, by separating qualities from the substance.

The only qualities of the *puruṣa* that Sāṃkhya will entertain are the eternal ones of beingness and consciousness, i.e., not the produced ones that are everywhere perceived as coming and going temporally, such as agential choice and desire, which cannot belong to an eternal entity. Apart from anything else, soteriological problems present themselves, from the Sāṃkhya perspective, if qualities are to be entertained as belonging to the *puruṣa*. Response to the charge directed against Sāṃkhya that liberation would be impossible in their changeless ontology of *puruṣa*, Sāṃkhya retorts that this very corollary is pertinent to the Nyāya position, not theirs. The above point can be understood from the following quote from *Yuktidīpikā*:

> If the qualities of agency and happiness were in the soul there would arise the undesirable consequence that *puruṣa* would not attain *mokṣa*. Because a quality can never be separated from its substance, if happiness and distress were the qualities of the *ātman*, there would be the undesireable consequence that the *puruṣa* could never attain liberation from them. Therefore, their being the qualities of the soul is not correct....therefore, it is impossible that the *ātman* has the qualities of desire, aversion, endeavour, *dharma*, knowledge, *saṃskāra*, which are of varied nature and mutually contradictory.[27]

Qualities such as agency and desire must belong to a substratum such as that proposed by Sāṃkhya: an inanimate and changeable *buddhi*, which can never

27. SK,Y, commentary to *Sāṃkhyakārikā* XIX, p. 148.

attain liberation as it can never be free from its inherent qualities, and so is distinct from the changeless *puruṣa*, which is not inherent to it.[28]

If *puruṣa's* eternality exempts it from any form of action, Sāṃkhya is now left with the problem of accounting for how an unconscious entity, *prakṛti*, acting purely mechanistically, can be an agent? In his preamble to the *kārikā*'s response to this problem, Gauḍapāda interrogates: "how can *prakṛti* which is non-conscious, act like the conscious *puruṣa*" and say: "I must provide the *puruṣa* with the objects of the senses in the three worlds like sound etc. and at the end liberation". Sāṃkhya offers in response a metaphor "just as the non-conscious milk functions for the nourishment of the calf, so does *prakṛti* function for the sake of *puruṣa*." [29] In other words, *prakṛti* just acts spontaneously due to the proximity with the *puruṣa*.

This fundamental changeless non-involvement of *puruṣa*, then, leads Sāṃkhya inevitably to the culmination of the *kārikās*: "no one, therefore, is bound, no one liberated: only *prakṛti* in her various evolutes transmigrates, is bound, and is released."[30] Gauḍapāda declares that: "it is the practice in this world to say the *puruṣa* is bound or liberated and all pervading. It is only *prakṛti* that is bound or liberated."[31] *Prakṛti* binds herself with her own virtues and vices

28. STK, Vācaspati on *kārikā* XVII, p. 78.

29. SK, G, Gauḍapāda on *kārikā* LVII, p. 70.

30. SK, LXII, p. 279

31.SK,G, Gauḍapāda on *kārikā* LXII, p. 74

(*bhāvas*),[32] and releases herself through them.[33] This is explained with the help of a metaphor that in war, victory or defeat should be attributable to soldiers. However, it is attributed to the king. Here, soldiers impersonate *prakṛti* and the king is the *puruṣa*.[34] In *Sāṃkhya Sūtras* as well as *Sāṃkhyakārikā* it is explained with the help of an example of a dance performer and audience. This analogy holds the key to our correct understanding of the discriminative knowledge. Let us imagine a situation where a dancer is performing in front of the audience. The audience witnessing the dance are intrigued and gets engrossed with the mesmerising performance. However, when the performance finishes the dancer goes off the stage then the audience are stirred back to their normal states. Here, the dancer represents the *prakṛti*, the dance performance represents its evolution, audience represents the multiple *puruṣas* and their dissociation represents the discriminative knowledge. *Puruṣa* misapprehends itself as the enjoyer and the agent.

In this regard Aniruddha considers an associated problem as 'if *pradhāna* (*prakṛti*) is the *kartṛ*, and *puruṣa* the *bhoktṛ*, then one entity would be experiencing the *karmic* consequences of acts performed by someone else.' The text and its commentaries do not engage the moral or judicial problem implicit in such a state

32. SK, LXIII, p. 279.

33. *Ibid*.

34. STK, Vācaspati Miśra on *kārikā* LXII, p. 122

of affairs, but concern themselves with establishing its possibility by analogy: "a non-agent can be the experiencer of results; just as is the case with food etc."[35]

In the manifestation of *prakṛti*, the association is between the *puruṣa* and the subtle body. This is the basis of the metaphysical error at the phenomenal level. The unconscious subtle body appears as if conscious and capable of undergoing experience, acquiring knowledge and doing actions. It takes itself to be willing, taking independent decisions, acquiring virtue and finally striving for moral perfection and liberation. On the other hand, the *puruṣa* appears as though an agent constituted of three *guṇas* and hence active. It assumes itself as the cause of change, capable of acquiring knowledge of the external world and aims for attaining perfection i.e. freedom from suffering. Thus, the agentship exists as long as the appearance of the association between *puruṣa* and *prakṛti* exists. What has been discussed is understood by Larson, in the words of Furtado as "according to Larson a double negation occurs here whereby contentlessness appears to have content and content appears to be conscious."[36]

Sāṃkhya justifies the ability to enjoyment *(bhoktṛtva)* of *puruṣa* by invoking agenthood. But this ability is due to the lack of discrimination between what is conscious and what is not.

In order to clarify the above point, Aniruddha states that:

35. SSū, A, i. 105, p. 61.

36. Vincent Gabriel Furtado, *Classical Sāṃkhya Ethics: A Study of the Ethical Perspectives of Īśvarkṛṣna*, Delhi: Media House, 2000, p. 68.

> The *puruṣa* is neither the agent nor the *bhoktṛ* (experiencer), but because of having the material nature[*prakṛti*] reflected in it, it has the notion of being the agent. It is because of not attaining the discrimination of the difference between *prakṛti* and *puruṣa* that the notion that it is the agent of the fruit of action comes about.[37]

In fact this metaphysical dilemma is resolved by Sāṃkhya by saying that *buddhi* is made of the finest potential of *prakṛti (sattva)*, which can attain a translucence equal to that of consciousness.[38] It is the *sāttvic* characteristics of *buddhi* which allow all human thoughts and experiences to absorb consciousness. When *buddhi* becomes conscious, that consciousness in turn is superimposed upon the *puruṣa*. From this the embodied *puruṣa* gets the idea of an experiencing person by mistaking the modifications of *buddhi* as its own.[39]

It is the association of the *puruṣa* and the *buddhi* in the agent (*jīva*) that gives one the self consciousness and the subjective experience of the world. By this association of *puruṣa* with subtle body, the former appears to have lost its perfection, innate purity and freedom. The quest of the agent/person is to gain freedom from the shackles and the bondage brought about by its association with the *buddhi*. The Yoga system tries to explain this bondage and gives an explanation for the self-realisation of the *puruṣa* in the individual *jīva* as will be explained in the next section.

---

37. SSū, A, i.106.

38. Rao, 'Perception, Cognition and Consciousness', p. 12, YS II.20.

39. Radhakrishnan, *Indian Philosohy,* pp. 268-9.

III

Prakṛti being the agent only in proximity with *puruṣa*, *buddhi* being the determinant and predispositions (*adṛṣṭa)* inhering in it, actions are performed by agents. A question may arise whether the agent is wholly determined by the prior active tendencies or whether there is also a sphere which is not determinate. *Yoga* philosophy explains as to how actions are done and how this activity of the *citta (buddhi and ahaṃkāra*) which is the seat of activity can be brought to a suspension of activity. Suspension of activity is to be understood in the sense of full control over one's actions. Patañjali defines *Yoga* as *cittavṛttinirodha* i.e. the cessation of the mental modifications and the union of an individual soul with the cosmic spirit or consciousness.[40] This function is the ability to stop at 'will' the fluctuations or modifications of the mind which is acquired through constant practice in a spirit of renunciation. Thus, two important features of *yoga* are worth mentioning here: there is the suppression at will of the modifications of the mind and these modifications are not causal but have been developed into a habit through constant practice, not for gaining a personal end, but in a spirit of renunciation.

But, this renunciation is not possible without any effort and volition. When the ultimate aim of the individual is to stop the modifications of mind then the obvious question that arises is about what brings about mental modifications. In order to understand the mental modifications, first of all it is to be understood

40. YS, 1.2, p.xxx.

what constitutes *citta* and its nature. Each individual self is complex whereby *prakṛti* comes in close proximity with self (*puruṣa)*. The *puruṣa* gets entangled with evolving *prakṛti* in the form of gross body and more closely related to a subtle body constituted of the senses, the manas, the ego and the intellect which are the evolutees of *prakṛti*. The intellect, ego and manas are together called *citta*. It is an internal instrument which serves the self within as its instrument.

The *citta* consists of several aspects; the desiring faculty is attributed to mind (*manas),* which gets attracted to outside things through the senses. Willing and discrimination is attributed to intellect (*buddhi)*, I-ness or the ego (*ahaṃkāra*) is the basis of individuality and the bed of memory which stores all the activities of the mind as fine impressions (*saṃskāra*).[41] They come to surface when appropriate conditions arise. So, mind (*citta*) is the internal organ with three functions, viz. cognition, conation and retention. The first two are knowing and willing while retention is the subliminal or latent impression.[42] Conscious functions of the mind like feelings or impressions of the things seen, of things retained, of things willed, of pleasure and pain felt are of the nature of *pratyayas* whereas *saṃskāra* or latent impressions are unconscious functions. Mind has two properties *pratyaya* and *saṃskāra*. Of these, *pratyaya* is called *cittavṛtti*. These mental modifications can be in the form of true cognition

41. Raju, *Structural Depths*, p.343.
42. YS, 1.5-6, pp. 17-20.

(pramāṇa), false cognition *(viparyaya)*, verbal cognition *(vikalpa)*, sleep *(nidra)* and memory *(smṛti)*.[43]

It can be further explained that these modifications are due to the afflictions (*kleśas*) which are the underlying and the fundamental cause of human misery and suffering. These are ignorance, egoism, attachment, aversion and clinging to life. The impressions of these modifications produce an afflicted state of mind and lead to the accumulation of *karma*. Of all the *kleśas*, ignorance (*avidyā)* is the root cause of the other four kleśas. *Avidyā* is not mere lack of knowledge but rather it is to be understood in the philosophical sense. In order to understand its meaning, it is important to recall the initial process whereby consciousness, the reality underlying manifestation, becomes involved in matter. Consciousness (*puruṣa*) and matter (*prakṛti*) are separate and utterly different in their nature. *Puruṣa* is intelligent, self sufficient and free whereas *prakṛti* is non-intelligent and unconscious. The self, which is eternally free and self sufficient, assumes the limitations involved with the association of matter. It is being said that on account of ignorance *(avidyā), puruṣa* identifies itself with *prakṛti*. It is only a form of the modification of the mind. When it is said to be eternal, it means that the flow of the modifications of the mind is eternal. It is rather non-awareness of reality. It is taking one thing for the other. Ignorance means taking a transient object as permanent, an impure object as pure, the

43. YS, 1.7-11, pp. 21-34.

painful as pleasant and the non-self as self.[44] It is the basis for the flow of all causes and for the corresponding latent impressions stored in the unconscious mind along with their *karmic* effects.

Afflictions *(kleśas)* in the form of ignorance, aversion, ego etc. form the reservoir of *karma* which bring about all kinds of experiences in present and future lives.[45] They are the underlying cause of the *karma* we generate by our thoughts, desires and actions. So every human life is like a flowing current in which the processes are at work simultaneously, the working out of *karma* made in the past and the generation of new *karma* which will bear fruit in the future. Each thought, desire, emotion and action produces its corresponding result with exactness and this result is recorded naturally and automatically in our life's ledger in the form of *karmāśaya* stored in *citta*. Patañjali explains that *karmāśaya* directly determines three factors of an individual's life: birth into specific life form, length of life and thirdly the nature of pleasant and unpleasant experiences to be experienced by the individual.[46]

Patañjali further elaborates that we are bound to the wheel of births and deaths on account of tendencies (*vāsanās)* which result in experiences of various kinds and these in turn generate more tendencies (*vāsanās)*. But this turns out to be one of those philosophical riddles which seem to defy solution. This process of

---

44. YS, 2.5, pp. 112-4.

45. YS, 2.12, pp. 121-2

46. Radhakrishnan, *Indian Philosophy*, p.315.

accumulating *saṃskāras* cannot be traced to its source because the 'will to live' or 'the desire to be' does not come into play with the birth of the human soul but is characteristic of all forms of life through which consciousness has evolved in reaching the human stage. In fact, the moment consciousness comes into contact with matter with the birth of *avidyā*, the *kleśas* begin to work and *saṃskāras* begin to form. Attractions and repulsions of various degrees and kinds are present even in the earliest stages of evolution-minerals, vegetables and animals and an individual who attains the human stage after passing through all the previous stages brings with him all the *saṃskāras* of the stages through which he has passed, though most of these *saṃskāras* lie in a dormant condition. So the whole process of the cycle of birth and death appears to be automatic. If this whole process of birth and death is cyclical and without beginning then the individual self will be an automaton. And if so, then who aspires for liberation? Actions are done by the agent and their fruits are reaped. Also an individual is responsible for his actions and gets rewards and punishments exactly in accordance with that. This gives an indication that an individual cannot simply be treated as automata as that will exclude responsibility of an agent.

In Sāṃkhya, freedom can be interpreted in the sense of the will, i.e., not to desire the unwanted afflictions, which perpetuate the path to renunciation (*nivṛitti)*. The volition here is the process of willing to free one self from the natural will to pleasure and enjoyment.[47] The yogic discipline of *yama* and *niyama* gives a way to curb these tendencies which have been developed through *saṃskāras*.[48] These tendencies can be changed and further accruing of the results of actions can be stopped. Thus, freedom of the agent constitutes in total control of tendencies like attachment (*rāga*) and aversion (*dveṣa*). The actions which are not done under the influence of these tendencies can be considered free. Here lies the scope of freedom of action on the part of the agent. These free actions pave the way towards the ultimate freedom. There is total cessation of the agent with the realisation of the *puruṣa* being all pervasive and not contained in the body in which it manifests. It is the absolute, unconditioned self.

The chapter may be summed up as follows: Sāṃkhya-Yoga does not ascribe agency to the self (*puruṣa*) which is eternal and immutable. They reject any argument which makes *puruṣa* an agent and prove that *prakṛti* is the only agent. But *prakṛti* being unconscious cannot be the self-initiated agent. This makes the explanation of agency a difficult point where the agent is said to be an embodied individual self (*jīva*). Again, within this *jīva,* the self appears to be an agent but really it is *prakṛti* in its evolutes possessed of *guṇas-sattva*, *rajas* and *tamas,* which is the agent. It is due to lack of discrimination that *puruṣa* seems to be an agent. The individual self limited by its psychical apparatus becomes the actor,

47. Bina Gupta, *An Introduction to Indian Philosophy*, New York: Routledge, 2012, p. 153.
48. Raju, *Structural Depths*, p. 345.

enjoyer and guide. It is an outcome of the proximity of the *puruṣa* with *prakṛti* where the latter gets animated by mere presence of the *puruṣa*. The agent has the 'freedom to' realise this misidentification. Freedom is interpreted in the sense of the 'will', not to desire unwanted afflictions, which eventually perpetuate the path to detachment. Thus, the agent has the 'freedom to' overcome by their own efforts tendencies like attachment and aversion to finally get 'freedom from' all three types of suffering which is tantamount to disentanglement of *prakṛti* and *puruṣa*. With this there comes the cessation of agency as well. Though previous actions determine the tendencies in an individual, there is also the power of making effort and trying to overcome these dispositions ascribed to the individual. This creates scope for freedom of action. Hence, it can be said that Sāṃkhya-Yoga accepts a compatibilist sense of freedom (both senses) bringing in the role of both determinism and freedom to ultimately bring about the dissociation of *prakṛti* from *puruṣa* (individual self) leading to ultimate freedom.

V

Karma, Agency and Freedom in Nyāya

The present chapter looks into the Nyāya concept of *karma*, agency and freedom. It will delve into the discussion of the nature of the agent (*kartā*), agency (*kartṛtva*) and questions that can be raised in the background of determination of one's life, its experiences by *karma* of past and present to address the issues of freedom of action. In this regard, the primary texts that will be referred to are the *Nyāya Sūtras* (NS) of Gautama with Vātsayāyana's commentary (NS,V) and the *Bhāṣā-Pariccheda* with *Siddhānta-Muktāvali* of Viśvanātha (BP,SM). Various secondary sources relevant to the topic of discussion will also be referred to. The Nyāya system of thought being a realist and logical school predominantly deals with the sources and ways of arriving at valid knowledge which finally leads to the realisation of the Truth. The aim of Nyāya philosophy is very succinctly put in the following words:

> ... logical criticism is not the sole or the ultimate end of Nyāya philosophy. Its ultimate end like that of the other systems of Indian philosophy is liberation, which means the absolute cessation of all pain and suffering. It is only in order to attain this ultimate end of life that we require a philosophy for the knowledge of reality, and alogic for determining the conditions and methods of true knowledge.[1]

1. Chatterjee and Datta, *An Introduction to Indian Philosophy,* Calcutta: Calcutta University Press, 2008, p.161.

I

The Naiyāyikas believe in the doctrine of *karma* strictly according to which, whatever is done must bear fruit. There cannot be loss of the effect of any action or deed (*kṛtapranāṣa*) till its effects are exhausted (being experienced by the agent). If there is no action, nothing happens or takes place (*akṛtābhyupagama*). *Karma* done in a particular life is accumulated and bears fruits in a subsequent life or lives. This accumulation of *karma* in the form of merit and demerit is an unseen potency (*adṛṣṭa*) which creates conditions for arising of the body and its conjunction with the soul.[2] But this unseen potency is an unintelligent and unconscious principle. Therefore, it requires a conscious principle i.e. God to supervise the entire operation of *karmic* retribution. It is usually observed that one does not get results in accordance with one's actions and expectations. Is it then absolutely in the hands of God to give deserts to the individuals according to his own will, such that individual's merit/demerit has no role to play?[3] It does seem so for the Naiyāyikas further deny that any individual gets rewards and punishments independently of God's observance. Keeping in view both positions it is accepted by the Naiyāyikas that God is the controller who supervises that beings get just deserts strictly in accordance with the moral quality of their actions. In other words, the results come in accordance with actions and that God supervises the process. In no case is the exacting law thus

2. NS, 3.2.70.
3. NS, 4.1.19-20.

compromised.[4] God observes that each person gets rewards and punishments strictly in accordance with one's good and bad deeds. This implies that whatever one does whether a good deed or a bad deed one has to bear the responsibility for the same. God envisioned as the *Adhiṣthātā* or the controller of the operation of *karma* is one of the causal factors involved in the production of the universe at the beginning of each cycle. So, the whole scheme of this world is ethicized. Further, the results are borne not in one life but they are carried to future births. It is evident that the doer of an action will be held responsible for actions done by them.

The notion/idea ofunseen potency *(adṛṣṭa)* must be looked at in more detail. Gautama in *Nyāya Sūtras* has a unified concept of *adṛṣṭa* in the form of merit and demerit (*dharmādharma*) inherent in the soul. It is a relation between the retributive efficacy of the deeds and amassed dispositions (*saṃskāras*) of the soul. But there is no doubt that *adṛṣṭa* becomes all-pervasive and that it functions as the key factor in re-interpreting the natural world as *saṃsāra* that is, as a mechanism of reward and punishment, or *karmic* retribution.[5] The conception of *adṛṣṭa* as a force determining the worldly existence of an agent is accepted by both Sāṃkhya and Nyāya. They also agree that it is the result of the accumulation of merit and demerit. But they differ on one very important aspect that is about the inherence of *adṛṣṭa* in the individual. According to Sāṃkhya,

4. Chatterjee and Datta, *An Introduction,* pp. 212-13, NS, 4.1.21.
5. NS,V, 3.2.71-72.

the *adṛṣṭa* resides in the subtle body which is the product of *prakṛti*. However, the *adṛṣṭa* as conceived in the Nyāya systemis absolutely free from any materiality. It resides in the self. Although in direct opposition to the Sāṃkhya doctrine, the Nyāya thinkers hold that the sense-organs are *bhautika* i.e evolved from matter, they admit a distinctly supra-physical principle as the 'efficient' cause of organic evolution. A foetus is, no doubt, developed from the seminal fluid of the parents; but the seminal fluid does not in all cases develop the foetus.[6] From this, the Nyāya thinkers argue that in order that foetus may grow out of the seminal matter, the hypothesis of *adṛṣṭa* is necessary. The *adṛṣṭa* is said to work in two directions upon the germinal substance. On the one hand, *adṛṣṭa* is inherent in the parents, a force which works upon the germinal matter of the parents towards the production of an offspring; on the other hand, there is *adṛṣṭa* of the future offspring, a pre-natal force, operating upon the parental germinal fluid, for its embodied emergence. According to the Nyāya philosophers no foetus can grow out of the germinal substance, without the operation of the bilateral *adṛṣṭa* and they contend further that each congenital peculiarity in an individual foetus is to be accounted for by the supposition of a corresponding peculiarity in the pre-natal *adṛṣṭa*.[7] In Sāṃkhya philosophy *adṛṣṭa* is held to be a force inherent in *ahaṃkāra* which is a materio-vital

6. NS, 3.2.70-71.

7. NS, 3.2.64, 3.2.69.

principle, tinged with a form of reflected consciousness.[8] The Nyāya way of thinking avoids this somewhat ambiguous position and points out in clear terms that *adṛṣṭa* is inherent in the *Ātman* or the conscious principle, which persists through its varied embodiments. To this embodied self, the Naiyāyikas attribute 'desire', 'aversion', 'effort', 'feelings of pleasure and pain', and 'cognition'. So, the *adṛṣṭa* attaching to the self and at the back of the organic evolution implies that all congenital developments of and peculiarities in the embryo are due to a pre-natal subconscious force, working upon the parental germinal matter, in accordance with its predetermined inclinations and tendencies.

Now a question may arise about why this concept of *adṛṣṭa* is important in the scheme of Nyāya philosophy. Like other schools of Indian Philosophy, Naiyāyikas also believe in the fourfold aims or goals of human life which are*artha*, *kāma, dharma* and *mokṣa* (*puruṣārthas*). Though there has been a controversy as to the addition of *mokṣa* as a separate category in the theory of *puruṣārtha* but let us set aside this issue like Rajendra Prasad does and accept that liberation is the ultimate goal of human life even for the Naiyāyikas.[9] *Mokṣa* in broad terms can be understood as the supreme end of life, freedom from the bondage of *karma*, freedom from the cycle of birth and rebirth (*saṃsāra*). It is a commonly accepted belief among almost all the propounders

8. S.N. Dasgupta, *Indian Philosophy*, Vol.1, Delhi: Motilal Banarisdass, 2010, p. 43.
9. Rajendra Prasad, 'Theory of *Purushārthas*: Revaluation and Reconstruction', *Journal of Indian Philosophy,* Vol. 9, 1981, pp. 49-76.

of Indian philosophy that what has existed prior to the present birth of their existing body i.e. the self or agent has existed beginninglessly. At this point, the fundamental question that arises is: how can the beginningless cycle of birth, death and rebirth be stopped? To this question the Naiyāyikas reply that by the exhaustion of merit and demerit *(adṛṣṭa)* of the agent, this cycle can be stopped which will eventually lead to the final release of the self from embodiment.[10] Thus it appears that the concept of *adṛṣṭa* brings about purposiveness in the world as it is one of the efficient causes of evolution. It is complementary to God who regulates and is the basis for the righteous sustenance of the universe.

II

According to the Nyāya School, the self alone is the agent. The Naiyāyikas argue that the material body is indispensable for the self. This means the self/consciousness requires embodiment. According to Nyāya there are two types of selves, the individual selves which are innumerable (*jīvātmā*) and an Absolute Self, which is one and infinite called God (*Paramātmā*), where both these kinds of selves are substances (*dravya*), which are eternal and all-pervasive (*vibhū*). There are certain qualities which are common to both these selves, namely emotion or desire, cognition, happiness and volition. Again, the qualities belonging to God are immutable, while those belonging to individual selves are temporal. Since our research is primarily dealing with the concept of

10. NS, 1.1.9.

agent, we will be only concerned with the exploration of the concept of individual selves (*jīvātmā*).

In *Nyāya Sūtra*, Gautama enumerates a list of objects of true knowledge (*prameyas*), and this list begins with the self. Vātsyāyana writes:

> ...here, the self is the seer of all things, enjoyer of all things, omniscient, experiences all things. Body is the place of its enjoyment and suffering. Enjoyment and suffering are cognitions (of pleasure and pain). The internal sense or *manas* is that which can know all objects. Action (*pravṛtti*) is the cause of all pleasure and pain; so also are the *doṣas* (defects), that is to say, passion, envy, and attachment. The self had earlier bodies than this one, and will have other bodies after this one — until "*mokṣa*" is achieved. This beginningless succession of birth and death is called "*pretyabhāva*". Experience of pleasure and pain, along with their means, i.e., body, sense-organs, etc., is "fruit" (*phala*). "Pain" is inextricably linked with "pleasure". In order to achieve *mokṣa* or *apavarga*, one needs to consider all happiness as pain whence will arise detachment and in the long run freedom.[11]

A *kartā* or an agent is commonly believed to be the one who performs an action. Not only that, but also this performer of the action should perform the action freely. This idea seems to be somewhat not abandoned in Nyāya philosophy. Gautama in *Nyāya Sūtra* says "no (i.e. the alleged defect of falsehood does not exist), because (the non-attainment of the results of the vedic injunctions) is due to the imperfections of the ritual performance, of the performer, and of the means employed."[12] It is clear from the *sūtra* that performer of the rite or the agent is responsible for an action. Another thing

11. NS,V, 1.1.9, Bina Gupta, *Cit Consciousness*, New Delhi: Oxford University Press, 2003, p. 40.

12. NS,V, 2.1.58.

which is made clear is that an agent must have a volition or desire to do an action. An action, prompted by volition is said to be voluntary action and one who performs an action voluntarily is said to be responsible for the same. The above can be understood with the following example to understand the meaning of voluntary action. Suppose I want to dive in the swimming pool. And if I do it while other things are constant then I will be the agent of that action. Now suppose it so happens that I am standing on the tip of the slide to jump and suddenly someone standing in the back loses his balance and accidentally pushes me. As a result of this I fall into the swimming pool. In this case, I would neither be considered as an agent nor held responsible for the same as the action is not guided by my volition but by something else which accidentally happened.

According to the Nyāya position, an agent (*kartā*) comprises of intentions, volitions and desires. This conception of agency is ascribed to self. It is worth mentioning here therefore, the characteristics of self. For Nyāya, consciousness is the attribute of the self, which is a substance. The self is eternal, real (*sat*), it is not one but many, and it can neither be created nor destroyed. Though consciousness is the quality of the self, it nonetheless is not its essential quality. The ultimate and emancipated self is devoid of consciousness. However, given the appropriate causal conditions available the self alone according to Nyāya is capable of having consciousness. The meaning is that when the self comes in contact with the mind, the mind with the senses, and the senses with the external objects, there is a conjunction which leads to the creation of consciousness in the self. The arising of consciousness in the Self can be figuratively described as through a chain of conjunctions which is as follows:

Self + Body + Internal Sense (*Manas*) + External Sense + External Objects

The summation of the above causal conditions leads to the emergence of consciousness. [13] According to the Naiyāyaikas, a pure or an objectless consciousness is inconceivable. The above discussion establishes the Nyāya conception of agent (*kartā*). For the Naiyāyikas agency is a special expression of the self's different capacities and potentialities, which coherently ties them together.[14] As mentioned earlier, the individual self/agent is a complex of body and self possessed of certain definite qualities such as virtue, vice, misery, aversion, happiness, cognition and residual trace.[15]

The specific focus of this discussion that is the nature of the agent can be elaborated further. Vātsayāyana, in his commentary on *Nyāya Sūtra* of Gautama, says that "the self is the knower of everything, enjoyer, and the perceiver."[16] Body and the senses are the locus of its enjoyment. Activity (*ceśṭā*), sense organs (*indrīya*) and object (*artha*) reside in a body, which is its substratum. These are the causes producing the body, the objects of senses,

13. Debiprasad Chattopadhyaya, *What is Living and What is Dead in Indian Philosophy*, New Delhi: People's Publishing House, 1977, p.409.

14. Matthew R. Dasti, 'Nyāya Self as Agent and Knower', *Free Will, Agency, and Selfhood in Indian Philosophy*, New York: Oxford University Press, 2014, p.113.

15. NS, 1.1.10.

16. NS, V, 1.1.9, pp. 20-23

knowledge, pleasure and pain. The agent undertakes action by motivation (*prayatna*) in the form of mind, body and speech activity. The agent is possessed of evil (*doṣa*). This incites the agent to act whether it is good or bad. Evils are of three kinds, attachment (*rāga*), aversion (*dveśa*) and mistaken ideas (*moha*).[17] The performance of these three activities under the influence of evil tendencies lead to accumulation of an unseen potency (*adṛṣṭa*) constituting of merit and demerit that determines the future birth.

Further the body in which the self abides is neither without a preceding embodiment nor without a succeeding one. The series of preceding bodies is without any beginning while the succeeding ones in the series terminate in liberation (*apavarga*). In particular, the burden of an individual's *karma* is held to be passed from one embodiment to another embodiment and to determine the particular form of rebirth the person suffers.[18] Both good and bad deeds create *karma*; even refraining from performing an action may add to the power of one's *karma*. Thus, one cannot attain liberation simply by doing good *karma*, rather one can attain it by doing those kinds of actions which do not increase the burden of merit and demerit and rather decrease or exhaust it.

Further, the agency of the self is clarified. It is said that the soul is the inspirer of the organs etc. for an instrument requires an agent (*ātmendrīyādyadhiṣthātā,*

---

17. NS, 1.1.18.

18. Karl H. Potter, (ed.) *Encyclopedia of Indian Philosophies. Indian Metaphysics & Epistemology: The Tradition of Nyāya-Vaiśeṣika upto Gaṇgeṣa*, Delhi: Motilal Banarsidass, 1977, p. 25.

karṇam hi sakartṛkam).[19] It is explained that self imparts sentiency to the sense organs and body and self is the agent which makes the sense organs work because they themselves are insentient. Moreover, the self is said to be the substratum of merit and demerit and not the body (*dharmādharmāsṛayoadhyakśoviśeṣaguṇayogataḥ*). [20] Had it been so that the body was the substratum of these, then the results of actions done by a particular body could not be experienced by another body. The existence of soul in another's body is to be inferred from its voluntary actions. [21] Voluntary movements are those movements which are a result of *pravṛtti* i.e. inclination. Knowledge, desire, effort etc. do not abide in the body and since voluntary movement is the outcome of effort, the self which is possessed of effort is inferred from its voluntary movements. So it is clear that the soul which is the agent is capable of doing voluntary or intentional actions. Body is the locus of the experiences of pain and pleasure. The experiencer is the agent (individual self).

A further claim made by Naiyāyikas is that the doer of an action and the experiencer of its results is the eternal self. Eternality of the self is proved by processes like remembrance etc. Gautama in *Nyāya Sūtra* gives an example[22] or examples as the case may be to explain this. He says a new born infant experiences joy, fear and sorrow and he cannot be said to have experienced

19. BP,SM, v.47,p. 65.

20. *Ibid.*, v. 49, p.78.

21. *Ibid.*, v. 50, p.79.

22. NS, 3.1.18,

those before, so how do these experiences happen? He answers that this can be inferred from the continuity of remembrance and this continuity can only be due to previous repeated experiences which could be possible only during a previous life. It follows that the personality continues to exist after the perishing of the body.

Further Gautama clarifies this by saying, "there is the desire for sucking the mother's breast on the part of the new born infant, which is inferred from its behaviour."[23] Such a desire is inexplicable without the habit of having had food in the previous birth. It is established that living beings are born as characterized and endowed by desire. Desire again is born of the recollection of the objects previously perceived. The previous perception of objects is not explicable without the admission of a body in the previous birth. Thus, the self recollects the objects perceived while having connection with a previous body and gets attached to those objects. It is evident that the self, as connected with the two bodies, undergoes rebirth. In this way the previous body presupposes a further previous body, which again presupposes a still further previous body and so on. As a result, the connection of the conscious self with the body is also without any beginning. Therefore, attachment is without a beginning and there is identity of the doer and the experiencer.

---

23. NS, 3.1.21.

In summary of the above points, it can be said that according to Naiyāyikas the agent is composed of self, body, mind, sense organs and sense objects qualified by consciousness. Agency belongs to the self and it is said to be the motivator of the sense organs. But this manifestation of agency belonging to the self happens when all the components are combined together as a complete whole. This is the prerequisite for the performance of actions, whether good or bad. An agent is innately endowed with desires for worldly pleasures and strives for their satisfaction. The desire for enjoyment etc. under the influence of tendencies impels an agent to do actions.

III

Now, one may enquire that if one is born endowed with desire then is there a cause of this endowment? To this Gautama answers that the cause of this desire is deliberation and anticipation.[24] Anticipation stands for the wish that one entertains for previously experienced things. Desire arises from the deliberation that such and such an object is the source of pleasure and pain. From this it is inferred that the desire of the just born baby as already discussed also originates from the recollection of objects previously perceived. As a matter of fact however, it is not yet proved that the self is actually produced nor do we find any other cause for desire than the said deliberation.[25] Desire is produced from the involvement with the object, which is the cause of reminiscent impressions

24. NS, 3.1.24.
25. NS, 3.1.26.

(*saṃskāra*). Also, a specific desire is due to a specific form of *adṛṣṭa* which is actually the cause of birth in a specific form. Thus, it is proved that desire doesnot have for its cause something other than deliberation. The underlying fact of the whole process of desire is that *saṃskāras* which are the impressions of the previous experiences of pleasure and pain determine or influence it. It has not been clarified in the *Nyāya Sūtras* whether the self or the agent has any control over the subsequent desires or that those are determined by the past impressions thereby leaving no scope for creativity. There is something very interesting being said about the agent, that is, this agent or the soul is intelligent and the guiding force of this agent's desires in the attainment of pleasure and avoidance of pain. So, the agent will choose those actions which bring about pleasure and escape pain. It seems probably that the Naiyāyikas have left some scope of freedom of the will here.

But as far as the ethical treatment of freedom of the agent and responsibility are concerned the analysis of the whole process of desiring or volition which gets translated into action is important. The Naiyāyikas do a psychological analysis of the volitional process. The psychological analysis of the will is a special feature of the Nyāya-Vaiśeṣika system. We can focus our discussion on Viśvanātha's analysis of volition in the *Siddhāntamuktāvali*. Viśvanātha has elaborately given the framework for the process of action in the following manner:

Cognition leads to Intention (cikīrṣā), which leads to volition (*kṛti*), and volition leads to physical effort (*ceṣṭā*) culminating in action (*kriyā*).[26]

He makes a distinction between volition or voluntary action and automatic or reflex actions of the organisms. The volition (*kṛti)* or effort (*prayatna*)[27] includes: the volition in the positive sense as conscious selection of the good (*pravṛtti)*, volition in the negative sense as rejection of the evil (*nivṛtti)*, and activities arising from the *jīvana* or life of the organism, in other words the automatic and reflex activities (*jīvanayoniprayatna)*. Effort can be voluntary or involuntary. Voluntary effort is the out come of the exercise of one's own free-will, actuated by desire and aversion (*icchādveṣapūrvakaprayatna*). Involuntary actions are the automatic reflexes where no volition is involved, i.e. those activities which are not brought about by one's own free-will (*svecchādhīnamatkṛtisādhya*).[28]

A well known exponent of Indian Philosophy, S.K. Maitra remarks:

> It is to be seen that by insisting on *svecchādhīnatva* or freedom as a necessary condition of volition the "Dinakari" excludes from volition proper not only the automatic and reflex activities of organic life but also all actions under blind impulse. It also follows from Dinakara's analysis that to constitute volition proper it is not sufficient that the action should be determined by conscious choice, in volition proper there being not merely conscious choice,

26. Dasti, 'Nyāya's Self as Agent and Knower', p. 115.

27. BP, SM, v. 149, p. 243.

28. *Ibid.*, v. 150, p. 243.

but also the consciousness that the choice has been free (*svecchādhīna*), i.e., determined by my own will.[29]

The analysis of the will or volition as set forth in the *Siddhāntamuktāvali of Viśvanātha* is not merely in its positive aspect as desire or attraction for the good (*cikīrṣā)* but also in its negative form as aversion and avoidance of the evil *(dveśa*). The conditions given for volition are said to be three in number. They are:

(i) The desire to do an action *(cikīrśā),*

(ii) The consciousness of a thing as capable of being done by oneself (*kṛtisādhyatājñāna*).[30]

(iii) The cognition that the action is conducive to one's own well-being (*iṣṭasādhanatājñāna*).[31]

Further, this consciousness of the wellbeing must be unaccompanied by a stronger evil (*balavadaniṣṭānubandhitvajñāna*).[32] This has been interpreted by Viśvanātha as not the consciousness of the absence of evil but the absence of the consciousness of evil. It is clarified that whenever we perform an action with a goal, we are pleased if we attain the goal. But for this we have to undergo some amount of exertion accompanied by pain. Still we do not withdraw ourselves from the action. This is because the pleasure which we get afterwards is not overwhelmed by the pain. If we realize that the pain of exerting would be

29. S.K. Maitra, *The Ethics of The Hindus*, Calcutta: University of Calcutta, 1963, p. 27.
30. BP, SM, v. 147, p. 241.
31. *Ibid.*
32. *Ibid.*

dominant to the pleasure to be attained, generally we would not have intended to perform the said action.

With the comprehensive analysis of volition now we proceed to discuss the conditions of aversion *(dveśa)*. Aversion like desire possesses positive and as well as negative factors. Aversion as a positive condition implies the awareness of evil which causes misery and as a negative condition the non-awareness of a greater good. Finally, after the deliberation on *dveśa* and *cikīrṣā*, the discussion of both the positive aspects of volition is relevant to discuss the Nyāya's conception of agency. Volition *(kṛti)* in the affirmative sense includes desire to do something *(cīkīrṣā)*, the cognition that it can be done *(kṛtīsādhyatājñāna)*, the cognition that it is conducive to the agent's good or the absence of the cognition of the stronger evil *(iṣṭasādhanatājñāna)*, the perception of the *upadāna*, matter or stuff out of which the thing is to be made (*Upādānapratyakṣa)*.

It is pointed out that since all these are the conditions of volition, therefore any one of them being absent; volition to do an action will not follow.[33] Hence, where the confidence in one's capability *(kṛtīsādhyatājñāna)* is lacking, there is no volition. This is why there is no willing of impossible things like producing rain or bringing the moon down to light the room. There is no volition for such things for they are recognized to be beyond the agent's power. Thus, realization of power must exist at the occasion of the willing: there will be no volition if

33. For the discussion of volition according to Nyāya-Vaiśeṣika see S.K. Maitra's *The Ethics of the Hindus*.

this realization of awareness is lacking at the time of willing though it may exist before or after it.

Similarly, where the consciousness of good *(iṣṭasādhanatājñāna)* is lacking, there is no volition. How then can one account for acts like suicide, what is their motivation? What can be the awareness of good in these acts of self-destruction? The reply to this can be given by saying that even in these there is awareness of good, for what happens in these conditions is that by finishing of one's life one can end one's suffering. On account of abnormal mental conditions there is a lapse of reason for the time being. For example, an individual with lack of awareness of good may resolve to take poison and commit suicide in order to escape a greater evil.[34]

If desire *(cikīrṣā)* is lacking then a hungry man would have taken some poisonous food intentionally. He does not take it, because though he has *kṛtīsādhyatājñāna* and *iṣṭasādhanatājñāna*, he does not have *cikīrṣā*.

While there is thus awareness of good in all volitions it is also necessary that the anticipated good must be relative to the time and circumstances. Thus what is good in one condition of life may not be a good in another condition and so may cease to be desired in the altered condition.

If the awareness of good is so important in producing a volitional action, the question arises, how can one explain the concept of moral evil? A possible

34. Jadunath Sinha, *Indian Philosophy*, Vol.1, Delhi: Motilal Banarsidass, 2015, p.679

answer that can be given is that, for the time being the person is unaware of the evil or he knows that stronger evil consequence will follow unless he does that action. Naiyāyikas give another explanation, that is, that the strong passion or immediate pleasure may make some people temporarily unaware of stronger evils. As a result these people indulge in forbidden acts.

Now, if we consider all the above mentioned conditions and the volition, which is the result of them, then it appears that the whole explanation presupposes that finite selves have volition *(kṛti)* only when they are embodied. Cognition, volition, pleasure, pain etc. are localized for each individual. Only when self is conditioned by a body, it becomes the locus of these qualities. Also, volition leads to physical efforts. Without these efforts volition cannot be translated into action. Thus, the body is an important factor in the whole process.

We can now discuss as to what extent the unseen power of merit and demerit determine the agent's freedom of action? An embodied being is born with desire which in turn is caused by deliberation of the past experiences of acquiring pleasure and avoiding pain. As has been already discussed self or the agent is inferred from voluntary movements that it makes which are said to be prompted by an agent's independent will *(svecchādīna)*. The conditions of voluntary actions or effort were enumerated as three and are, the desire to do, the notion of a thing being feasible through one's effort, being productive of what is desirable i.e. conducive to the good of the agent, and the perception of the material.

Following from preceding discussions, we can make some important observations pertaining to the issue of freedom of the agent. The Naiyāyikas on the one hand accept the determination of present life experiences by the unseen potency generated through the past life *karmas*. On the other hand, they give a psychological explanation of the voluntary performance of the actions. This implies that even if one is determined by the merit and demerit, still there is a scope for freedom of action, for one is free to will, choose, and perform actions. Here freedom can be understood in the sense that the agent is fully determined by its own will and not from extraneous factors. Thus, it can be said that I am determined by my own tendencies, by my own impulses, by my own reason. But I have also the 'freedom to' voluntarily, i.e., by my own 'will' choose and perform actions. This satisfies one of the essential requirements of ascribing moral responsibility that one's choice is not coerced. In a nutshell, the action becomes an intentional action which in turn brings about moral responsibility and this shows the compatibilist understanding of freedom in Nyāya. Also, with this sort of voluntary activity an individual self (agent) can achieve 'freedom from' pain and rebirth leaving the self in it's natural state without any qualities which is called *apavarga*.

Now, after an indepth analysis of the Nyāya conception of agency in the light of freedom and *karma*, we can draw some conclusions.

Naiyāyikas accept a strict relation between the moral quality of actions performed and the fruits that a person bears. The merit and demerit one accrues forms an unseen potency (*adṛṣṭa*), which resides in each individual self. But the unseen potency being devoid of intelligence cannot guide the dispensing of the results of actions on its own. Therefore, Naiyāyikas accept God as the moral administrator who supervises the moral order. The bearer of *adṛṣṭa* is explained by Nyāya as a combination of the soul, body, mind, sense organs and the external objects. Out of all these the self alone is capable of acquiring consciousness; however, this can happen only when it is in concatenation with the body. The embodied self is regarded as the agent, doer and the source of all the voluntary actions. The embodiment of an individual self is indispensable for the manifestation of agency. Knowledge, desire and effort are inherent in an agent. The framework of the action to be done is that desire (*ichhā*) is caused by the self, desire to do leads to the will (*cikīrṣā*) to do, the will to do leads to the effort (*prayatna*), effort leads to action (*karma*).[35] It is also evident that the agent who has volition to do actions but is ignorant of the means for its realisation cannot be an agent. In the same way, a person who is ignorant and does not desire cannot become an agent. Also, one who desires, but because of laxity, does not make an effort, can also not be an agent. This sort of performance of the action of the

35. J.N. Mohanty, 'Intentionality and Theory of the Qualities of the Soul' in *History of Science, Philosophy and Culture in Indian Civilization,* Centre for studies in Civilizations, Delhi: Motilal Banarsidass, 2008, p. 248.

agent without any external constraints creates scope for the freedom of action. Thus, the Naiyāyikas endorse a voluntarist view of the freedom to act within the compatibilist model.

VI

Karma, Agency and Freedom in Advaita Vedānta

This chapter explores the questions of agency and freedom from the point of view of Advaita Vedānta philosophy. This promises to be an intriguing exploration for the very reason that Śaṃkara believes that action cannot bring about liberation. It is knowledge that is sufficient for attaining the Truth, quite unlike most other schools where action plays a pivotal role in the process of release.[1] If action in Advaita is ineffectual from the ultimate point of view then the question arises: Does action has any role to play as far as reaching the knowledge of the ultimate is concerned? Śaṃkara's views appear to be inconsistent with the ultimate import of the *Upaniṣads*. But he found a way to negotiate between the position which considers action to be real and mandatory for achieving release, and from the one that considers action to be redundant for attaining ultimate freedom or *mokṣa*. To do so he described two levels of reality namely: empirical reality *(vyāvahārika sattā)* and transcendental reality *(pāramārthika sattā)*. So, instead of seeing one which is very much a matter of empirical experience in contradiction with the other i.e. transcendental, Śaṃkara ingeniously handled the situation with the play of *avidyā*. This also addresses the very understanding of the Upaniṣadic aphorism '*Tat Tvam Asi*' or 'I Am That' that signifies there is a being who has to realise 'That' i.e. the

1. By 'other' schools is meant both orthodox and heterodox schools of classical Indian philosophy except Cārvāka.

existence of an individual who is going to be awakened by the knowledge of *Brahman* (*Brahmavidyā*) and which is simply un-negetable. Thus, a basic understanding of Śaṃkara's Advaita thought is required. This will help to understand the concept and importance of agency, if any, in his scheme.

Advaita or the non-dualist tradition of Vedānta cannot be said to be synonymouswith Śaṃkara's thought only. Though he has been a very influential as well as impressionist thinker of Advaita thought, the roots of it can be traced back to pre-Śaṃkara commentators on *Vedāntasūtras* of Bādarāyaṇalike Upavarśa (before A.D.200), Brahmanandin (dates unknown), Draviḍāchārya of 'the South' (dates unknown), Sundara Pāṇḍya, Gauḍapādāchārya (A.D.600) of North Bengal. Śaṃkarāchārya (A.D. 725) of Kerala was also followed by his pupils Maṇḍana Miśra, Padmapāda, Sureśvara, Toṭaka and Hastāmalaka (all belonging to A.D. 680-750).[2] For the present chapter my focus would lie mainly on the selected portions of the commentary of Śaṃkarā on Bādarāyaṇa's *Brahmasūtra* (BSsbh). Apart from this I will also be looking at a number of secondary texts with varying interpretations of Śaṃkara's views.[3]

---

2. Karl H. Potter, *Encyclopedia of Indian Philosophies: Advaita Vedānta upto Śaṃkara and His Pupils*, Vol.3, Delhi: Motilal Banarsidass, 1981, pp. 18-19.

3. I have used Swami Gambhirānanda's translation through out the chapter unless otherwise specified.

I

Like many other schools of Indian philosophical thought, Advaita Vedānta also talks about the final aim of the human life which is the realisation of *Brahman*. It is the final deliverance and awakening of the truth that 'I Am That' or 'That Thou art.'[4] The idea of liberation from bondage has been unanimously accepted and explored by all the systems of Indian philosophical thought. What leads to bondage i.e. being in the cycle of birth and death, is ignorance, which in turn leads to the misidentification of the individual self from what it really is. Śaṃkara explains the cause of bondage to be *avidyā* (ignorance) which is the root cause of this misidentification. This, through the knowledge of *Brahman,* can be dispelled resulting in the awareness of the Self or *Brahman*. The word '*Advaita*' which literally translates as non-dual needs attention. Śaṃkara maintains that there is no distinction between the seeker (subject) and the sought (object). Individual self and Self (*Brahman*) are non-dual. But this distinction remains when the individual is engulfed in ignorance. For him, the knowledge that: "*Brahman* is alone true, and this world of plurality is an error, the individual self is not different from *Brahman*,"[5] frees a person of his acquired individuality to finally immerse into the ultimate reality.

4. *Aham brahmāsmi,* (*Br.* I.iv.10)

5. Reiterating the *Upaniṣadic* truths as given in *Brahmajñānavalimāla*, verse 20 (trans. S.N.Sastri). http://www.celexvel.org/adisankara/brahmajñānavalimāla.html accessed on 28 May 2017.

If the ultimate aim of any individual is to attain non-duality and that is the absolute truth, then the question arises about why the individual is caught in the sphere of apparent duality which he has to transcend. Śaṃkara explains it by way of the connection of the individual self with the *antaḥkaraṇa* which he says is eternal as he accepts *māyā* (cosmic ignorance) at the general level and *avidyā* (ignorance) at the individual level to be eternally present deluding the individual self. But this reality of *māya* is denied from the absolute point of view as according to Advaita thought *Brahman* is the only reality.

Śaṃkara explains that any individual under the sway of *avidyā* is bound to act. His actions are very much an outcome of a misidentification. He is not able to differentiate between what truly is and what is merely apparent. When his actions are limited by the reality of the *vyāvahārika sattā* (empirical reality) there is a sense of his being an agent. This sort of agency makes him liable to act and accrue the results of the actions done which he has to bear in a future course of life or lives.

Karl Potter writes, while explaining the cycle of birth and death which is a perpetual outcome of actions done by the individuals (agent) in their lifetime according to Śaṃkara, that an individual (*jīva*) is primarily a gross body composed of material elements, sense organs, motor organs, mind (*manas*), ego (*ahaṃkāra*) and internal organ (*antaḥkaraṇa*). These form the substratum of an individual's capacity to engage in conscious sensibility and subsequent activity.

Secondly, he has with these an aggregate of past *saṃsakāras* or tendencies i.e. the remnants of actions performed by the individual (*jīva*) in previous lives, which have not started to fructify (*vīpāka*).[6] These *karmic* remnants are talked as of three types: (i) *prārabdha karma, karmic* remnants that are pre-determined at the time of birth which will successfully work out in the given or present life time. (ii) *sañchita karma*, the *karmic* deposits of the actions done in the present life time. (iii) *sañcīyamāna karma,* consequences of the actions performed in the present lifetime which will mature in the future lifetime.[7]

When *karmic* remnants start to fructify, they, under the sway of dispositions to act, determine firstly, the manner in which the potential *karma* will in fact be actualised; second, the nature of experience of pleasure or pain (*bhoga*) that will accrue to the performer of actions; and third, the accumulation of the future *karmic* residues which will further determine actions in the future. These tendencies (*vāsanās)* come out in the form of decisions arrived at by the internal organ (*buddhī* or *antaḥkaraṇa*) to get certain kinds of results. These tendencies can be either pure or impure. At any moment in one's conscious lifetime one is guided in acting by such tendencies, which develop into desires (*kāma*).[8]

---

6. Karl H. Potter, 'Karma Theory in Some Indian Philosophical Systems', *Karma and Rebirth in Classical Indian Traditions*, (ed.) Wendy D. O'Flaherty, Delhi: Motilal Banarsidass, 1981, p. 249.

7. N.Veezhinathan, 'The Nature and Destiny of the Individual Soul in Advaita', *Journal of the Madras University,* Vol. 47 No. 2, 1975, pp. 19-20.

8. This discussion of the play of *vāsanā* is utilized by Potter in his discussion of theory of *karma* from K.S. Iyer's article on 'Ethical Aspects of the *Vedānta*',*Vedānta Kesari* 3, 1916-17, pp. 39-41.

It has been explained in the *Upaniṣads* and Śaṃkara also follows these explanations as to what happens to all these organs at the time of death and what transmigrates. The speech function gets absorbed into *antaḥkaraṇa* or *manas*.[9] Similarly other functions of the respective organs get merged into *manas*.[10] After this, *manas* absorbed of these functions gets absorbed into breath (*prāṇa*).[11] This *prāṇa* gets merged with the individual self (*jīva*),[12] i.e., with the internal organ as limited by the awareness, *karmic* residues and *vāsanās* present at the moment, a man physically stops breathing. The *jīva* thus impeded joins the five *tanmātras* corresponding to the gross elements- earth, water, fire, air and ether.[13] The cluster of the five subtle elements provides a subtle body (*sūkṣama śarīra*) which encloses the *jīva* with its adjuncts, just as the gross body did during life. All these factors gather in the 'heart'. The *jīva* at this point is filled with awareness, *karmic* residues, *vāsanās*, desires and the internal organ is capable of consciousness which is completely controlled by past *karmas*, since the external sense organs have stopped functioning. At this moment the *jīva* conditioned by its *karma*s develops a tendency (*vāsanā)* which determines the direction in which the subtle body will go as it leaves the heart, which point of exit it will take, by what path and what kind of birth it will eventually

---

9. BSsbh, IV.ii.1
10. *Ibid.*, IV.ii.2.
11. *Ibid.*, IV.ii.3.
12. *Ibid.*, IV.ii.4.
13. *Ibid.*, IV.ii.5.

proceed to.[14] The subtle bodies can follow one out of the three paths: northern path (the way of Gods), southern path (the way of fathers) and Yama's world (*saṃyamana*) based on their actions and knowledge of God. Śaṃkara clarifies that the individual self who is an agent of actions creates a link from the old body to the new one by means of its *tendencies*.[15] And the whole path of travel is explained as to how self encased in its subtle body goes from one birth to the other passing through different planes. In this process what is required from the point of view of my study is the understanding of the distinction between the will determining tendencies and *karmic* residues, for this will help us to better apprehend the deterministic implications of the doctrine of *karma*. These tendencies are an agent's determination in the form of desires to aspire for certain goals or objectives. Any of these tendencies is the effect of one's *karmic* residues. So, if one's *karma* is pure, then one's tendencies will be pure. Impure *karma* will lead to impure *vāsanās* which in effect brings about painful experiences and less happier experiences. This is how actions done in the past determine the experience one will undergo in future.

Potter, with precision clarifies that one need not be worried about the absolute determination of oneself by these tendencies as they are only some of the conditions which will be playing a role in doing actions in one's life. There need not be this as the only relation between the cause/causes of one's actions

14. *Ibid.*, IV.ii.16.

15. *Ibid.*, III.i.1.

and determinations. Again, *vāsanās* can be one of the causes of one's orientation towards something but this might not be strictly the only one. So it seems to be a loose relation. This has implicit in it the scope of freedom to act on the part of the agent. Potter explains it by way of constructing an argument. The result of any action done (*saṃskāra*) in one life need not necessarily determine an event in another life. It merely creates a tendency or a disposition on the part of the agent which may or may not materialise into action. So, there is a gap between possessing a disposition and its translation into action. This gap opens the way for overcoming or trouncing these tendencies. When an agent becomes conscious by way of the knowledge of the scriptures of these dispositions to act, he can practise restraints and perform yogic exercises to neutralize these tendencies and develop detachment in doing actions. So, the individual self or agent can attain release (*muktī*) during one's life time. K.R. Rao writes that "Vidyaranya in his *Jivan-mukti Viveka* asserts that *jivan-mukti* (embodied liberation) is the direct result of cessation of instinctive propensities (*vāsanās*) achieved by the negation of the routine mental activities (*mano-nāsa*) and consequent realization of pure consciousness and true knowledge (*tattva-jñāna).*" [16] This according to Potter creates scope of freedom for the performance of actions for the agent where actions are not performed under the

16. K.R. Rao, 'Perception, Cognition and Consciousness in Classical Hindu Psychology', *Journal of Consciousness Studies,* Vol. 12 (3), 2005, p. 17.

influence of any instinctive dispositions but with the knowledge of the ultimate.[17] More on this is included in the third section of the chaper.

This is the path of *karmayoga* understood from the side of *jñāna yoga* or *niṣkāmakarma*. When actions are performed not under the influence of emotions of attachment or hatred but with the conscious awareness born out of the knowledge of the ultimate reality, there arises detached action.[18] It gives the doer a better sense of freedom to act for one knows that one's doing an action will in no way bind the agent to further consequences of the action done. Such an understanding in a way gives the gist of the Advaita thought that once the discrimination is realised between the subject (self) and everything other (object) than that, there emerges an awareness which dispels ignorance of misidentification.

Activity or action (*karma*) remains an integral part of the life of the individual self until one gets release from the supposed reality of the empirical plane. The primary meaning of the word '*karma*' in Advaita is action only and the other meanings of it are born out of the implications of the consequences of the actions done. They may be bodily, mental and vocal, or those that are enjoined by the *Vedas* and prohibited by the *Vedas*. Within the enjoined there may be obligatory day to day life duties (*nityakarma)*, occasional obligatory duties like performing rites on special days (*naimittikarma)*, duties done for the fulfilment

17. Potter, *Encyclopedia of Indian Philosophies*, pp. 20-30.

18. This sort of action is one of the principal teachings of *Bhagvada Gītā*.

of desires (*kāmyakarma)* and expiatory actions (*prāyaścitakarma*). A duty implies here performance of actions. The performance of these duties is important according to Śaṃkara "not for the fruition of the knowledge, but for the emergence of knowledge itself."[19] According to Śaṃkara, performance of each action (*karma*) has the potentiality of producing *karmic* residues which, in the future, condition birth in a particular species, span of life, and the kind of experiences of pleasure and pain the *jīva* will experience in the next life after death. Not all the results of the action lead to fruition in one life and they may show their effects in several life times.

Potter writes:

> Śaṃkara thinks that in general the more intense and proximate residues, whether sinful or meritorious tend to mature first, but that the general rule here is subject to many exceptions because there are incompatibilities among several residues which have equal claim but only one of which can mature at a given time.[20]

This can be more clearly understood by looking at Śaṃkara's explanation for the maturation of *karmic* residues. He quotes from *Chhāndogya Upaniṣad* "Among them those whose conduct has been good (*ramaṇīyacaraṇaḥ*) will quickly attain some good birth... Again those whose conduct has been bad (*kapūya caraṇaḥ*) will quickly attain bad birth...".[21]It is further clarified by Śaṃkara that those (i.e Mīmāṃsakas) who think that the individual selves

19. BSsbh., III.iv.26.

20. Potter, *Encyclopedia of Indian Philosophies*, p. 31.

21. BSsbh., III.i.8, p. 567, (Ch. V.x.7).

exhaust all the results of their *karma* done in worldly life through enjoyment in heaven or suffering in hell and return back to earth without any remnants of *karma*, are not correct. For, only those results get fructified which were meant to be experienced by the doer in heaven or hell, the rest will have to be experienced by the individual self without exception till one gets liberated with the knowledge of the ultimate reality.[22] Also, it is not the case "that death induces all unfulfilled results of work to become ready to yield fruits."[23] Śaṃkara citing the *smṛti* explains that any *karma* can lie dormant for a long period of time when it is clogged by another *karma* of opposing consequences. Thus, there is no necessary relation between the time of performance of action and its fructification. And, if all the latent *karmas* become activated at a single death and thus lead to a single birth, then since scriptures deny for any possibility of acquiring fresh *karma* in heavenly or hellish life; therefore, there cannot arise any merit or demerit.[24] And in the absence of that no further birth is possible. But, this is not the case. Selves after experiencing the pleasures of heaven and sufferings of hell do come back on earth to fructify their preserves of *karma* till they attain liberation/release.

This process of maturation can be understood as: performance of the action in life A at time T can bring effects to the same agent in life B at time T2 or for

22. BSsbh., III.i.8, p. 569.

23. *Ibid.*

24. *Ibid.*

that matter at any other time Tn+1. This can produce three different types of experiences, be it pleasurable, painful or indifferent.[25] Further, any action done in one life time which produces an *apūrva*[26] (unseen potency) to work out its results in other life times on its own is not acceptable to Śaṃkara. He interprets *Bādrāyaṇa's* view to show that an unintelligent thing (*apūrva*) cannot produce effects on its own and accepts God to be the organizer who dispenses the results of actions keeping in conformity with merits and demerits accrued by the *jīva* or the agent.[27]

Even though the conditions or situations might be arranged by God but that does not in anyway restrict or absolutely determine the doings of a doer. The relation between past *karma*, present experiences and the future is not absolutely fixed as there may be so many permutations and combinations of which we are neither fully equipped nor capable of making concrete sense. Thus, we cannot say that there is a determined relation between an action 'x' done in life A, its residue producing *vāsanā* in life B which leads the agent to do an act 'y', which produces evil but is immediately accompanied by pleasant experience. This indeed happens most of the times but it goes beyond our understanding, for God doesnot generally give experiences of results of action based on their being

25. Potter, 'Karma Theory in Some Indian Philosophical Systems', p. 258.
26. Mīmāṃsā accepts this.
27. BSsbh., III.ii, 38-41.

virtuous or vicious as many times the performance of a good deed may be accompanied by pain. He rather bases it on the merit and demerit of past acts.[28]

Thus, Śaṃkara's understanding of *karma* does not see it as an inexorable law with no scope of any alterations etc. and one has to go beyond it to becomerealised. For him, till the time the knowledge of *Brahman* in not realised actions are performed and they are predecessors to the realisation of *Brahman*. But the truth is that the agent in the midst of worldly life acts and has to understand that this life of action is not the ultimate truth and the agent has to pursue the knowledge of the ultimate about who they actually are.

II

We, now proceed to analyse the notion of agency in Advaita philosophy with the following intriguing questions. Who is the agent/doer according to Śaṃkara? Does the doer have any ontological status? For according to Śaṃkara individuation is the outcome of *adhyāsa* whereas there is no real independent existence of the individual self from the transcendental point of view. The whole explanation as well acceptance of actions and its results by him on the one hand and rejecting the reality of their existence from the transcendental point of view raises questions for accepting doer along with the possibility for release. Also, is there any freedom available to the doer for overcoming the effects of actions done previously?

---

28. *Ibid.*, III.i.8.

In the very beginning of his *Brahmasūtrasbhāśya*, Śaṃkara, clarifies that there is a distinction between the subject and the object, and when the knowledge of this distinction is not there then there is superimposition of one on the other i.e. the *antaḥkaraṇa* and others[29] are superimposed on the self. Similarly, one superimposes on the internal organ etc. the self which is opposed to the non-self and which is the witness of everything. This superimposition does not have a beginning and is eternally present. Due to this, there is an appearance of the manifested universe and its apprehension, there is agentship (*kartṛtva*) and enjoyership (*bhoktṛtva*).[30] In order to disillusion and clarify to a person about this superimposition and giving the knowledge of the unity of the individual self with the ultimate reality i.e *Brahman*, there begins a discussion about the nature of the self. Thus, at the very onset of the enquiry into the nature of *Brahman*, the purpose is clarified to be the knowledge and awareness to the agent/doer (*jīva*) who is also an experiencer (*bhoktā*) and is the ultimate self or *Brahman* and due to eternal ignorance there is the non-realisation of this identity.

We must also seek answers to the various objections that have been raised with regard to the Advaitin acceptance of doership only at the phenomenal plane and rejection of doership from the ultimate point of view. Śaṃkara is usually criticized for not recommending ethical actions as a way to realization, as for him it is only knowledge which is sufficient for the release. If knowledge is the

29. *Citta, buddhī, ahaṃkāra, manas etc.*

30. BSsbh., 1.i.1, p. 6.

only requirement then is it not the case that the performance of actions becomes redundant? It may be so but even then the following four practices (*sādhana catuṣṭaya*) have been prescribed in Advaita Vedānta by way of which one should prepare oneself for the life of realization. These four are and consist in: (i) the ability to discriminate between what is eternal and what is transient, (ii) the giving up of all desires for enjoyment here and hereafter, (iii) development of the qualities of the control of mind, speech etc. of detachment, patience and endurance, and the power of concentration, (iv) the desire for liberation (*mumukṣā*). [31] It is further clarified that for attaining liberation from the world of bondage due to action, the path of action is not important as what one can attain by way of that is heaven. It can be important only as a means to purify one's mind (*citta śuddhī)* and prepare it for the reflection of the self. But ultimately it is the path of knowledge that will lead to release of the sense of ego and individuality; and attainment of the awareness of unity. So, action precedes the attainment of the knowledge of the ultimate truth i.e. *Brahman*. This gives us some scope to talk about agency in Advaita thought though from the point of view of ultimate reality there is no agent. Still at the phenomenal level (*vyāvahārika sattā*), as one is first of all aware of oneself in this sphere, there is the need for understanding one's status here. One's physical existence is the outcome of one's actions in previous births and one is absolutely ordained to this cycle of birth and death, to pain and suffering unless one

31. P.T. Raju, *The Philosophical Traditions of India,* Delhi: Motilal Banarsidas, 2009 p. 187.

releases oneself with the knowledge of the ultimate. It would be preposterous to reject the existence of this sort without an inner realization of its illusoriness which cannot happen unless one exists at the phenomenal plane. Also, to be kept in mind are the problems that will be there to deal with at the phenomenal level by declaring everything to be illusory, Śaṃkara clarifies that it is important to understand the nature of doer/agent and only then one can realise what it is not. So, the method that is adopted by Śaṃkara is that he first attributes all sorts of existence of worldly things and then goes for subsequent retraction.[32]

Another question that can be asked is what about the claim that *Brahman* is the originator, sustainer, and destroyer. Is there some sense of agency attributed to *Brahman* as well? Agency it seems cannot be ascribed to *Brahman* from the point of view of ultimate reality as this appearance of *Brahman* as the creator et cetera is due to *adhyāsa* (superimposition). One of the main objectives of the inquiry into the nature of *Brahman* is to clarify the sense of doership available to an agent whereby it is not at all indicated that one has to cease action physically. It is infact indicated that the knowledge of the ultimate truth makes one give up the sense of doership/agency. In what way is the awareness of oneself not being an agent to be looked at? In order to get a better grasp of the issue one has to remind oneself that Śaṃkara accepts *satkāryavāda* theory of causation along with *vivartavāda* i.e. the effect exists in the cause and there is

32. A.J. Alston, *The Methods of the Vedānta,* Delhi: Motilal Banarsidass, 1997, p. 43.

no real transformation of the cause into effect.[33] Keeping these in mind one can make better sense of the sort of agenthood Śaṃkara is ascribing to the self. Again, it is not merely self per se but the self under the sway of ignorance; that is an agent. Thus, the discussion of issues pertaining to agency would not be relevant if causation is not accepted, which the case is with Advaita thought. This is because from the ultimate point of view these (agency/causation) have no ontological status. Whether agents are autonomous or free would be meaningless if there are no agents to start with. Advaitins accept the self or *Brahman* as the metaphysical precondition of the subject-object duality. This duality is because of the superimposition *(adhyāropa)*. Nothing can negate *Brahman* as the very act of negation signifies that there is a subject who negates it. Keeping this in mind Śaṃkara tries to construct the possible explanation for subject-object duality and explains it as constituting phenomenal reality. Acceptance of this sort of practical approach to provide a coherent picture of the world, has behind it various reasons for Śaṃkara. He first gathers whatever has been attributed of this world as existent and then explains it by way of analogies that it is not but the play of *avidyā* which creates this world picture in front of you and is nothing other than, and over and above, *Brahman*.

To accept only the ultimate reality or *pāramārthika sattā*, the *vedic* teachings and others like hearing of scriptures *(śravaṇa)*, reflection *(manana)* and

33. Chatterjee & Datta, *An Introduction to Indian Philosophy*, Calcutta: Calcutta University Press, 2008, p. 368.

profound meditation (*nidhidhyāsana)* would be of no use and there would have been no need for these three as there would be neither bondage nor any sort of creation. Also, levels of reality have been talked of by him give a coherent and systematic explanation to the world, its origination and destruction along with the beings liable to birth and death. This implies that straightaway talking about the absolute reality without taking the physical world of experience into consideration could have brought various attacks on the rationality of Advaita thought. The very motive to know and realize the ultimate makes sense for a person who is put into this worldly life, who can eventually make a difference between the eternal and the non-eternal, and nurture a desire to know the ultimate. Thus, topics like agency and freedom to act make sense only at the conventional level and this level of reality is the only platform to talk about it for ultimately this is also false for Śaṃkara.

Śaṃkara compares the world to the show of a magician, to explain how *Brahman* is the cause of the world.[34] As the magician projects various things in front of the audience which are taken to be real by them when witnessing them, similarly this world (the created one) is a mere projected reality, which in fact is illusory and has no independent ontological status. As has been said before, Śaṃkara has utilized *vivarta* theory of causation to show the apparent transformation and no real transformation of cause into effect. Space and fire metaphors are used by him

34. BSsbh., II.i.1.

to explain these.[35] To say that sparks of fire are different from fire would be erroneous as sparks are particles of fire only. They are same in essence. Similarly, when we see differently placed things they give us the appearance of divided space but in actual space is one. Also, when ever such terms as *pariṇāma* or creation (*sṛṣṭi*) are used, they rather understand it in the sense of *dṛṣṭisṛṣṭivāda* that it is like perception of a hare's horn which does not exist.

Śaṃkara has vehemently opposed the Sāṃkhya doctrine of *prakṛtipariṇāmavāda* and it has been one of the major concerns for him to show how unconscious *prakṛti* can be the agent and *puruṣa* is *dṛṣṭā* as well as *bhoktā*. *Prakṛti* causes as well as undergoes real transformation. Sāṃkhya school claims to be in direct continuation of the *Upaniṣadic* philosophy. If this is so, then there was a major challenge before Śaṃkara to defend *ajātivāda* i.e.the theory of non-origination in consonance with the *Upaniṣadic* teachings. Śaṃkara rebutted the Sāṃkhya account of creation, along with their theory of actual transformation of *prakṛti* i.e. *pariṅāmavāda*.[36] He raised various objections which question the insentient *prakṛti* to be the cause of the world like: i) the inferred one (*pradhāna/prakṛti*) is not (the cause) owing to the impossibility of explaining the design. ii) the inferred one cannot be the cause, since the tendency to create (cannot logically arise in it). iii) If it be claimed (that *pradhāna* acts spontaneously) like milk and water, then even here (intelligence is the guide). iv) And (*pradhāna* is not the

35. *Ibid.*, II.iii.43.

36. *Ibid.*, II.ii.1-10.

cause) since (nothing extraneous to it exists, so that) it has nothing to rely on (for impulsion to or stoppage from action). v) And *pradhāna* cannot change (automatically) like grass etc. (into milk in a cow) for such a change does not occur elsewhere (eg. in a bull). vi) Even if (spontaneous modification of *pradhāna* be) accepted, still (*pradhāna* will not be the cause) because of the absence of any purpose. vii) If it be argued that like a (lame) man (riding on a blind man) or a loadstone (moving iron), (the soul can stimulate *pradhāna*), even then (the defect will persist). viii) Besides, *pradhāna* cannot act on account of the impossibility of (the existence of) any relationship of the principal and its subordinate (among the *guṇas* constituting *pradāna*). ix) And even if the inference be pursued otherwise (still the defect will persist) owing to the absence of the power of intelligence (in *pradhāna*). x) And (the Sāṃkhya doctrine is) incoherent because of the contradiction involved.[37]

Thus, in the above *sutras* Śaṃkara questions any argument that is given by Sāṃkhya for treating *prakṛti* to be the cause of creation like what could be the purpose for the unconscious *prakṛti* to bring about creation? There is nothing in the *guṇas* constituting *prakṛti* which can explain any self initiated activity in it lest any purpose for creation. It is not acceptable to Śaṃkara that an action can be brought about by something unconscious, since the performance of any action involves conscious agent. And as far as the Sāṃkhya explanation of action by way of proximity of the *puruṣa* (consciousness) with the *prakṛti*

37. *Ibid.*

(matter), Śaṃkara rejects this theory as for him nothing or no event can be brought about by mere proximity of an agent. Śaṃkara attacks the Sāṃkhya strategy of explaining creation with the reflection of *puruṣa* in *prakṛti*, because of which *prakṛti* actually starts real transformation, with the milk metaphor. It is like that the grass turns into milk without a cow or in proximity of a cow. But this cannot happen until the conscious agency of cow is accepted here. If the milk automatically flows out of the udder of the cow to nourish the calf (Sāṃkhya view), one should not forget that cow as conscious element is involved here who desires for the same.[38] Śaṃkara also gives magnet metaphor to calm the Sāṃkhya objection. Just like magnet doesn't move itself but moves anything having iron properties similarly *Brahman* without itself undergoing any change brings about creation and is the single principle behind it.[39] This upholds the monistic model of Advaita thought where *Brahman* manifests itself in the form of so called real world (i.e. *vyāvahārika sattā*) just like gold is made into different ornaments,[40] similarly, there is no real, actual transformation of *Brahman* into something, it is merely an appearance of modification for Śaṃkara. Everything is essentially *Brahman*. This can be explained thus, the *Brahman* appearing as the world is like the rope appearing as snake. The rope (*adhiṣtāna*) never changes. The rope is never affected by the distorted

38. A.J. Alston, *Śaṃkara on Rival Schools,* Vol. IV, London: Shanti Sadan, 1988, pp. 182-83.

39. BS bh., II.ii.2.

40. BSsbh., I.iv.23, 6.1.4-5; Mackenzie C.Brown, *Hindu Perspective on Evolution: Darwin, Dharma and Design,* Routledge, 2012, p. 27.

perception of the snake on it. It is merely one thing appearing as though it were another. The *Brahman* merely appears as though it were the world.[41]

The problem for the Advaitins, then, is to describe everyday experience where the effects come from causes, there are agents, events happen which do not seem to be illusory and are so real. Śaṃkara first tries to describe creation by maintaining *Brahman* as the ground/source of all relations. With this position the result would be, since the self is nothing but the *Brahman*, it will be self-governed in manifesting or creating the world of common-sense experience. To justify this, he had to distinguish sentient from the insentient.[42]*Brahman* being pure consciousness, how can the origination of insentient things in the world be explained from the conscious source, for a thing cannot produce something which is opposed to its very nature? For e.g. an apple tree cannot produce cabbages. Śaṃkara replies to the Sāṃkhya objection "that this world cannot have originated from *Brahman* on account of the difference of its character is founded on an absolutely true tenant,"[43] by saying "that from man, who is acknowledged to be intelligent, non-intelligent things such as hair and nails originate, and that, on the other hand, from avowedly non-intelligent matter, such as cow-dung, scorpions and similar animals are produced."[44] But, one may

41. 'World' here can also mean *jīva* or the agent or the empirical self. (Ma,G),p.105.(Śaṃkara's commentary on *Kārikā* 12 of *Vaithathya Prakaraṇa.)*

42. All this is to rebuke *Sāṃkhya* position that something unconscious is the agent or the cause of creation.

43. BSsbh., 2.1.6., p.305, (Thibaut tr.).

44. *Ibid.*, p. 305.

object that with this example the relation of *Brahman* to the world cannot be explained because cause and effect have some common properties by way of which they are related while this is not the case as far as *Brahman* and the world are concerned. Śaṃkara replies that both *Brahman* and the world share a common characteristic of Being or *Sattā*.[45] Again, it may be objected that if the objects of enjoyment (the insentient world) passes over into the enjoyer (*Brahman*) there would result non distinction between the two.[46] So, the doctrine of *Brahman's* causality must be abandoned as it would lead to the sublation of the well established distinction between the subject and the object. To this Śaṃkara clarifies, that such a distinction may still exist as one experiences in common day to day life. Just like foam, ripples, waves, bubbles etc. are different modifications of the sea, consisting of water, are non-different from the sea, still amongst themselves these are perceived actions and reactions in the form of separating or coalescing. The foam, wave etc. do not loose their individuality in relation to one another, even though they are modifications of the sea and non-different from it, which is water. And even though they do not loose their individuality in one another, they are never different from the point of view of their being the sea.[47] So is the case with *Brahman*. Similarly, pot, which is different from the clay and out of which it is made, gets recycled back

45. *Ibid.*, p.306.

46. BSsbh., II.i.13, p.324-6.

47. *Ibid.*

into the elemental substance without maintaining its individual identity.[48] Cloth metaphor[49] is also utilized to describe the distinction between the cause and the effect comparing *Brahman* as the efficient cause of the world to the spread cloth. Just as cloth remains hidden in its cause viz. yarn and becomes distinctly known when acted upon by agents like shuttle, loom, weaver etc., similarly *Brahman* is said to be rolled up cloth and creation to be the spread cloth. Thus, the difference is only in the form not in essence.

The discussion of creation has been very intricately dealt with by Śaṃkara for, he, time and again in *Brahmasūtra Bhāṣya* reminds the reader that creation is for the one who has not realized *Brahman*, creation is merely an appearance, everything is *Brahman*. Śaṃkara's preceptor's preceptor Gauḍapāda in his Gauḍapādakārikā mentions that no *jīva* is ever born in anyway. There does not exist any cause which can produce it. This is the highest Truth, that nothing is ever born.[50] With ignorance one sees the distinction between oneself and the ultimate. *Brahman* is not really the creator in the sense of agent/doer from the ultimate point of view. All the discussion about *Brahman* undergoing transformation or modification or moving into the creation have been rejected by Śaṃkara, and metaphorical language is used to make sense of and understand the appearance of the world which the beings inhabit. So, *Brahman* becomes

---

48. *Ibid.*, II.i.21, p.347.

49. *Ibid.*, II.i.19, p.345.

50. (Ma,G), p. 224. (Śaṃkara's commentary on *Kārikā* 48 of *Advaita prakaraṇa*).

both an originator and non-originator at the same time. He is originator from the point of view of empirical reality (*vyavahārika sattā)* and non-originator from the point of view of transcendental reality (*pāramārthikasattā)*. Similarly, the individual self or the phenomenal self is said to be identical to Brahman in essence. The whole discussion about creation is important because it gives clarity about Śaṃkara's treatment of oneness of *Brahman* and the individual self (*jīva*). And it is only a matter of appearance that agency is ascribed to the individual self.

And as it has been discussed earlier that something insentient cannot be the cause of the creation, and then if there were any creation, and the self is the cause of it, then it has to undergo transformation/ modification. On account of *Upaniṣadic* teachings, Advaitins believe in the identity of the *Brahman* with the embodied being in the text "Having created that, He entered into that" (*Tai*. II.VI) where it is said that *Brahman*, the creator, entered into the body, without undergoing any modification"[51] i.e. it became one with the embodied being. If this is so then the creatorship of *Brahman* will actually belong to the individual/embodied self. And "being an autonomous agent the self might be expected to produce only what is beneficial to itself and not things of a contrary nature..... for we know that no free person will build a prison for himself, and take up his abode in it."[52] This objection is answered by Śaṃkara as *Brahman* being spoken of as the creator of the universe

51. *Ibid.*, II.i.21,p.347.
52. *Ibid.*

is by nature eternally free, why will it have faults like doing something beneficial or harmful. Nor does its knowledge and power have any limits for it is omniscient and omnipotent. But the individual self is not of that kind meaning that faults can arise of not doing what is beneficial or otherwise. So, individual self is different from the *Brahman*. Once again, it might be objected that "has not the declaration of non-difference also cited as in "That thou art" (Ch.VI.viii.7) and similar texts?"[53] To this Śaṃkara responds that various analogies have been cited in the *Upaniṣads* like that of cosmic space and space in the pot etc. to grasp the idea of non-difference. The *jīva* is not something other than the Self, as the space in the pot is not other than the space itself. The *jīvas* originate from the *Brahman* just as the space-in-pots originate from space. When the pot is destroyed, the space within the pot is merged into space itself. In the same way *jīva* are merged into *Brahman* when ignorance is removed by the right knowledge. Also, when one is awakened to the reality of 'That Thou Art' then the transmigratory nature of the individual self is removed along with the creatorship of *Brahman*; "Then, in that state where can creation come from."[54] Till the time the individual self is under ignorance, there arises difference between *Brahman* and the embodied self and to this embodied self "the superiority of *Brahman* is known from the texts like, 'He is to be sought for, He is to be inquired into' (Ch.VIII.vii.1)".[55] Thus, creatorship or agency does not belong to *Brahman*. An interesting point comes here. When we

53. BSsbh, II.i.22, p. 348.

54. BSsbh, II.i.23, pp.349-50.

55. *Ibid*.

mean *Brahman* by the term 'self', then it is eternally free and has no agency, but if this term 'self' is used for the embodied self (*jīva*), then it is bound by its own consequences producing actions. Bothways, in the usage of the term 'self' there is nothing outside of it (self) that determines its agency. Agency of the agent is not guided by or influenced by factors external to the doer. But, creation and agency have relevance only from the point of view of empirical reality. This in a way alerts us to understand the illusory nature of both and affirms the oneness of *Brahman* and the world (creation and agent) for, it is only when one wakes up from sleep that one realises the falsity of the dreams. As the reality of dreams disappear after waking up, so is the world known to be illusory when one attains the knowledge of the ultimate. Thus, by way of *apavāda* or the method of rejection/retraction Śaṃkara denies the agency to the self.

It can further be argued that if neither *Brahman* nor the individual self are agents and it is conjunction of the internal organ (*antaḥkaraṇa)* and other organs with the self that brings agency, then one can say that internal organ (*antaḥkaraṇa)* may be the cause of the world, i.e., the mind as the agent can be attributed its own agency. Śaṃkara does not accept this position. In the section on 'Agent'[56] (*kartā*), he gives arguments to press that the internal organ or the cognitive faculty cannot be the agent. Along with denying agency to the internal organ he says that individual self is the agent for which the following arguments are advanced:

56. BSsbh, II.iii.33-39, pp.494-97.

(a.) The individual self must be an agent, otherwise injunctive sentences in the *Vedas* become purposeless. Scriptures enjoin various duties for an agent whose presence is a reality, and those sorts of injunctions can have no sense if there be no soul with agentship.[57]

(b.) Soul is the agent other than the cognitive faculty *(antaḥkaraṇa)* in accordance with the *Upaniṣadic* teachings that it roams about in the intermediate state of dream.[58]

(c.) Again, the individual self is described as an agent for it controls the organs and retains all the information gathered by the cognitive faculty.[59]

(d.) The cognitive faculty is not the agent for then there will be reversal of the roles and power where something (*antaḥkaraṇa*) which is instrumental in performing actions will become the agent. If the cognitive faculty becomes the agent then the distinction between the cognizer and the means of cognition will go away.[60]

(e.) If empirical self is not the agent then the state of *samādhi* as taught in the *Upaniṣhads* for the realization of the self will not be established, for in that state there is total cessation of the activity of the cognitive faculty and who can be witness to that state, if the empirical self is not the agent.[61]

---

57. *Ibid.*, p. 494.

58. *Ibid.*

59. BSsbh, II.iii.35; Br, II.i.17; Br, II.i.8.

60. BSsbh., II.iii, 36-38.

61. BSsbh., II.iii, 39.

Thus, Śaṃkara not only tries to establish the agency of the individual self at the phenomenal level, but also willingly accepts it as a level of reality to be known and understood for it to be finally rejected from the transcendental point of view. It is clarified that due to the superimposition of the adjuncts (*upādhis*) on pure consciousness because of ignorance as well as one's past life impressions (*vāsanas*), one takes one's agency as well as one's ego to be the real individual. When one is in such a world view and tries to know who one really is, then there comes an inner awareness for what one is not. This paves the way for one's realization. But before one reaches that stage self's conditioned existence is to be accepted. This conditioned or embodied existence of the self better known as *jīva* has agency (*kartṛtva*) ascribed to it.[62]

Further, Śaṃkara tries to establish the self's agency through argument for *pramā* and *pramāṇa*. He says a knower is an agent in regard to knowledge and in that capacity is independent. This independence lies in the fact that an agent is not subject to the processes and operation of instrument i.e. the internal organ, sense organs and the body, but is itself the regulator as well as controller of all these. It is the knower who puts means of valid knowledge to use and the instruments cannot become active on their own without the agent (knower) inciting them to activity. Also, it is the case that the Self in itself is unchangeable, eternal and intelligent. It never undergoes any transformation, and activity is not inherent in

62. *BrahmaSūtra-Catuḥsūtrī*,(tr.),Vidyasudhakara Pandit Har Dutt Sharma, Delhi: Chaukhamba Sanskrit Pratisthan, 2005, p. 24.

it by nature. So, how does this activity takes place? Śaṃkara explains that it is by the way of mutual superimposition between the self and the non-self.[63] Mutual superimposition is explained to understand the outcome of it as activity. If valid knowledge is merely the function of internal organ alone without any sort of involvement or support of consciousness or intelligence, then this would lead to no cognition because internal organ is unconscious. Therefore, the functions arising from it will also be of the same nature. And if valid knowledge is all pure, then it would require no knower for its *āśraya*[64] and this would result in the uselessness of the sense organs as well.

So, valid knowledge is the outcome of the modification of the internal organ, reaching out to the object to be known, is intelligent by nature and resides in the agent.[65] But, how could this internal organ be of the nature of intelligence if the intelligent conscious self were not superimposed on it? Again, how can there be individual self as agent, independent of the internal organs superimposed on the self? Thus, with reciprocal superimposition, there results cognition with the individual self as the knower as well as the agent.

Śaṃkara's engagement of his thought at the phenomenal level indirectly points towards his position on agency of the phenomenal self with the following statement:

---

63. *Ibid.*, p. 25.

64. *Ibid.*

65. *Ibid.* p. 26.

> ...in the actual perception the soul is independent, since it is endowed with consciousness. Moreover, the soul is not wholly independent in the matter of activities yielding results, for it has to depend on particular space, time and cause. An agent does not cease to have its agentship just because it has to depend on accessories; for a cook can very well be a cook even though he has to depend on fuel, water etc. and because of a diversity of the accessories, it is nothing contradictory for the soul to engage in an irregular way in activities yielding good, bad and indifferent results.[66]

From the above discussion it is evident that the embodied self (*jīva*) is the agent.

Thus, a clear distinction is drawn by Śaṃkara for the independence of the individual self with regard to cognition and action. As far as cognition is concerned a self is fully autonomous whereas when we talk about action, the agent/individual self is not fully independent due to the limiting conditions like space, time, cause, situations etc. but still that does not take away the agency from the agent, for e.g. as discussed above a king is the agent in war as far as his soldiers are fighting on his behalf or a cook remains a cook even if various other things which are required for the manifestation of his being a cook remain missing. Moreover, it is not necessary that the individual self always does actions producing beneficial results; it can perform all sorts of actions yielding favourable, unfavourable and indifferent results. This clearly shows that Śaṃkara in a way accepts some sort of determinism in the production of an action but it is not that strong whereby an individual self is turned into a puppet. The ascription of agency to the individual self even in the absence of auxiliaries

66. BSsbh, II.iii.37, p. 496.

for its exemplification hints or rather opens a way for ascribing responsibility to an agent for the actions performed by him.

Thus, an agent enjoys agency and autonomy only at the phenomenal level where he/she is under the sway of *avidyā* or ignorance. But when he actually becomes free i.e. self realised then this autonomy to act ceases as then there is no agent left.

III

As it is clarified in the previous discussion that the individual self (*jīva*) is both the doer of the actions as well as experiencer of the consequences of the actions done at the phenomenal plane, Śaṃkara accepts the law of *karma*. It is not possible for anyone to escape the fruits of one's *karmas*. As mentioned in section I, meritorious deeds bring about merit and bad deeds bring about demerit; these form a collection which in turn determines the tendencies of life experiences like, birth, place, status, and so on. If an individual self is so determined by its *karmas* then is there any scope for it to improve upon its future existence? More clearly, does an agent have any freedom in the sense of freewill to act? And even if there is freedom to act, is there any use of it when ultimately it is by way of knowledge that one realises one's true self rather than by action? This problem is relevant because in Advaita the whole of *vyāvahārika* experience, as explained earlier, is due to *avidyā*; all activities including all willings are due to it. The sense of agency itself is a product of *adhyāsa*. Such being the case, the injunctions like 'you ought to do good', 'you should not do evil' etc., may appear quite meaningless. Being a monist Śaṃkara denies any freedom to action from the ultimate point of view but still it can be accepted. In doing the latter Śaṃkara ensures that he is in tune with the *Upanisadic* passages. It may be said that there are passages in the *Upaniṣads* which advocate both determinism and free will. Ranade writes that the *Kauṣitaki Upaniṣad* which is one of the oldest of the *Upaniṣads* depicts "man as a puppet in the hands of God who makes him do good as well as evil action. This one truly indeed causes him whom he wishes to lead up from these worlds to perform good action. This one also indeed causes him whom he wishes to lead downward to perform bad action."[67]

In *Chhāndogya Upaniṣad* it is said that there is no real freedom for man before he acquires *ātmajñāna*. "Those who go hence without here having found the soul (*Ātman*) and those real desires (*satya kāma*), for them, in all the three worlds there is no freedom. But those who go hence, having found here the soul and those real desires, for them in all worlds there is freedom."[68] Various passages in the *Upaniṣads* reflect an acceptance of man's free will. In *Kathopaniṣad*, it is said,

> the better (*śreyas*) is one thing and the pleasanter (*preyas*) quite another. Both these of different aims bind a person. Of these two, well is it for him who takes the better. He fails of his aim who chooses the pleasanter.' Again, 'both the *shreyas* and the *preyas* come to a man.

67. R.D. Ranade, *A Constructive Survey of Upaniṣadic Philosophy*, Bombay: Bhartiya Vidya Bhawan, 1986, p. 229.

68. *Ibid.*, p. 230.

> Going round the two, the wise man discriminates. The wise man chooses the better, rather than the pleasanter. The stupid man, for getting and keeping (*yoga kśema*), chooses the pleasanter.[69]

Answering the question 'from where does this body come?' the *Praśnopaniṣad* says that the *prāṇa* comes to the body by the acts of the mind.[70] Similarly a statement of the *Bṛhadāraṇyaka Upaniṣad* goes like – "As his desire is, so his will; as his will, so is the action that he performs, as his action, so is the fruit that he procures for himself."[71] Thus we see in the *Upaniṣads* both the denial and the affirmation of freedom of will and action. These instead of being seen as opposed and contradictory to each other have been accommodated together by Śaṃkara. He says, God is the dispenser of the fruits of one's actions but he doesn't do it independently of his own will. While dispensing the fruits of actions He takes into account the merit and demerit of the each individual self (agent).[72] So, ultimately it is individual's own actions which is a necessary condition for determining his future. But again all this is relevant till the time one doesn't attain release (*muktī*) because ultimately from the metaphysical point of view all this is illusory for Śaṃkara.

To sum up the chapter we can say that for Śaṃkara actions are an outcome of the misidentification of the *jīva* under the influence of ignorance *(avidyā)*. The

---

69. A.K. Sharma, 'Freedom of Will and Action in Shankara's Philosophy', *Vedānta Kesari*, 2011. (file:///E:/books/Freedom%20of%20Will%20and%20Action%20in%20Shankara's%20Philosophy%20_%Advaita%20Academy.html) accessed on 13 December 2016

70. *Ibid.*

71. Ranade, *A Constructive Survey,* p. 229.

72. BSsbh., III.ii, 41.

association of ignorance and the individual self is accepted as beginningless. Actions thus performed lead to the accumulation of *saṃskāras* generating *vāsanās* or tendencies. This in turn determines one's present as well as future existences. The performance of good and bad deeds leads to the formation of pure and impure tendencies respectively. Further, all the effects of *karma* have to be borne by the individual self. The existence of human life at the phenomenal level is accepted as a gateway to the realization of the ultimate Truth. It is not possible to comprehend the self directly. Hence, one proceeds from the known to the unknown. Duality, then ceases to exist when the highest Truth is known. Another distinctive feature of Advaita philosophy is the acceptance of the fact that actions donot lead to liberation. The *jīva* imagines himself a doer as well as the enjoyer. The self which is pure does not possess action etc. and is not attached to the sequence of cause and effect. However, there is a distorted perception of himself as an individual like a misperception of a snake on the rope. It is only knowledge of the truth 'I Am That' and its realization which leads to the giving up of individuality. All the actions are accepted only at the empirical level to be finally rejected from the transcendental point of view. When the truth is realized there no longer remains any distinction between the knower, knowledge and the known. Śaṃkara uses the method of attribution to the subsequent retraction *(adhyāropa-apavāda)* to know the nature of Self. However, this is also a fact that an individual undergoes the whole process of bondage and liberation. This implies that agency has to be taken into account even if it has to be given up from the ultimate point of view. Śaṃkara accepts the embodied being (*jīva*) to be an agent distinguishing it from the Sāṃkhya conception of agency being ascribed to *prakṛti*. He explicitly states that an unconscious entity like *prakṛti* cannot be the agent. For him the cognitive faculty (*antaḥkaraṇa*) unless driven by the individual self cannot become an agent. Again, if the cognitive faculty is the doer then instead of being the instrumental cause it will become the efficient cause of the action, which cannot be the case. Thus, nothing apart from the individual self (*jīva*) can be the agent according to Śaṃkara. The acknowledgement of agency at the empirical level further leads to the question of the performance of actions by the agent. Whether an agent is free or not is consistently handled by Śaṃkara. Keeping in view the *Upaniṣadic* import, Śaṃkara accepts the autonomy of the doer at the practical level, where individual selves though being determined by the past life impressions and tendencies still have the freedom to reform their actions for the good. But ultimately this autonomy subsides with the cessation of the doership when one realizes real freedom. It can be said that Śaṃkara's view seems to have an affinity to a compatibilist sense of freedom of the agent where agent(s) is free to purify their minds even when they are determined by their past *karmas*. Individuals with their own efforts dispel ignorance and with knowledge of *Brahman* realize the true Self, that is to say, the agent has the 'freedom to' get 'freedom from' ignorance (*avidyā*) to be one with the ultimate reality, i.e., *Brahman*.

CPSIA information can be obtained
at www.ICGtesting.com
Printed in the USA
LVHW080951220123
737613LV00013B/1044

9 781805 455141